$4.50

MW01290770

May the Lord richly bless you. In Him

William J Hill

FUNDAMENTAL

FACTS

FOR

FAITHFUL

FOLLOWERS

William F. Hill

Holiness Literature International
PO Box 263
Independence, IA 50644

www.holinessliterature.com

ISBN-13: 978-1466298415
ISBN-10: 1466298413

Printed in the United States of America.

All scripture quotations are from the King James Version of the Bible. Bold emphasis done by the author.

CREDIT PAGE

A Special Thanks to Tracy Keller for proofreading and typing.

TABLE OF CONTENTS

FOREWORD

But though we, or an angel from heaven, preach any other gospel unto you than that which we have preached unto you, let him be accursed. Galatians 1:8

What kind of man would dare make a statement such as the Apostle Paul made in Galatians 1:8?

To pronounce someone accursed, or doomed and damned, just because they might happen to preach something different from what he preached seems to be the epitome of haughtiness, if not bigotry.

Does this man who claims to be an apostle of Christ honestly believe that he has a corner on the gospel?

Might it be that the ruler Festus, when he said, ". . . Paul, thou art beside thyself: much learning doth make thee mad," was more discerning than we had previously thought?

One thing we may be sure of, if Paul is accurate, a multitude of preachers both today and in times past are in a lot of trouble.

Let me hasten to say I believe Paul was taking into account all other individuals who had a part in writing the Holy Bible when he used the words, ". . . than that which **we** have preached unto you." We can see this in his following words:

All scripture is given by inspiration of God, and is profitable for doctrine, for reproof, for correction, for instruction in righteousness:

That the man of God may be perfect, throughly furnished unto all good works. II Timothy 3:16, 17

Paul was not concerned that the other writers of the scriptures were in error, rather, he knew there would come those who would attempt to subvert the gospel. Listen to his words.

Take heed therefore unto yourselves, and to all the flock, over the which the Holy Ghost hath made you overseers, to feed the church of God, which he hath purchased with

7

his own blood.

For I know this, that after my departing shall grievous wolves enter in among you, not sparing the flock.

Also of your own selves shall men arise, speaking perverse things, to draw away disciples after them.
Acts 20:28-30

In this book, I will use the words of many who were used of God to bring the Bible to us; however, I will focus a great deal of attention on Paul's writings.

We have so many different opinions on things we really should agree on, because we often do not like to believe that which is clear.

Again, Paul:

Preach the word: be instant in season, out of season; reprove, rebuke, exhort with all longsuffering and doctrine.

For the time will come when they will not endure sound doctrine; but after their own lusts shall they heap to themselves teachers, having itching ears;

And they shall turn away their ears from the truth, and shall be turned unto fables.
II Timothy 4:2-4

As we begin this book, let us once again hear from Paul.

Study to shew thyself approved unto God, a workman that needeth not to be ashamed, rightly dividing the word of truth.
II Timothy 2:15

As we said before, so say I now again, If any man preach any other gospel unto you than that ye have received, let him be accursed.
Galatians 1:9

1
SALVATION

As I begin this chapter, I feel a sense of awe come over me. Can any subject be more precious to the redeemed child of God than his or her personal salvation?

The Hebrew word **yeshowah** and the Greek word **soteria** are translated into our word **salvation.** When we look at the Hebrew and Greek words, we find they cover a lot of territory. They mean "rescue, safety, deliverance, health."

The experience of salvation — being redeemed, converted, born again, or whatever you may choose to call your experience of being saved from a sinful life and embarking in a new life in Christ — is at once, both child-like in simplicity and yet profound beyond belief.

We have seen the hardest of people — bound by drunkenness, drugs, or a host of other things — come to Christ in simplicity and child-like faith, pray a simple prayer of repentance, many times weep scalding tears of sorrow over a previously wasted life, then leave that place of prayer entirely transformed and delivered from every habit and sin.

How can we explain that to the unbeliever? After all, the unbeliever is incapable of understanding and comprehending the greatness of our salvation and of our God. Why, Paul?

But if our gospel be hid, it is hid to them that are lost:

In whom the god of this world hath blinded the minds of them which believe not, lest the light of the glorious gospel of Christ, who is the image of God, should shine unto them.   II Corinthians 4:3, 4

Again, the Apostle Paul has so much to teach us. Many Christians, all over the world, use his writings as a guide and pattern to witness to unbelievers to lead them to salvation. Consider what is commonly called "The Romans' Road."

1. Recognize that all have sinned:

As it is written, There is none righteous, no, not one.
Romans 3:10

For all have sinned, and come short of the glory of God.
Romans 3:23

2. Realize there is a penalty for sin:

For the wages of sin is death; but the gift of God is eternal life through Jesus Christ our Lord.   Romans 6:23

3. Understand that God has made a way:

But God commendeth his love toward us, in that, while we were yet sinners, Christ died for us.   Romans 5:8

4. Believe and confess unto salvation:

That if thou shalt confess with thy mouth the Lord Jesus, and shalt believe in thine heart that God hath raised him from the dead, thou shalt be saved.

For with the heart man believeth unto righteousness; and with the mouth confession is made unto salvation.

For the scripture saith, Whosoever believeth on him shall not be ashamed.

For there is no difference between the Jew and the Greek: for the same Lord over all is rich unto all that call upon him.

For whosoever shall call upon the name of the Lord shall be saved.   Romans 10:9-13

That is simple gospel, or good news of God's plan for man. What simplicity and yet what power.

For I am not ashamed of the gospel of Christ: for it is the power of God unto salvation to every one that believeth; to the Jew first, and also to the Greek.   Romans 1:16

Countless numbers have stumbled over the utter simplicity of God's plan. Others have resented, even mocked, because they wanted something complicated, difficult, or something that would boost their ego.

For the preaching of the cross is to them that perish foolishness; but unto us which are saved it is the power of

God.

For it is written, I will destroy the wisdom of the wise, and will bring to nothing the understanding of the prudent.

Where is the wise? where is the scribe? where is the disputer of this world? hath not God made foolish the wisdom of this world?

For after that in the wisdom of God the world by wisdom knew not God, it pleased God by the foolishness of preaching to save them that believe.

For the Jews require a sign, and the Greeks seek after wisdom:

But we preach Christ crucified, unto the Jews a stumbling-block, and unto the Greeks foolishness;

But unto them which are called, both Jews and Greeks, Christ the power of God, and the wisdom of God.

Because the foolishness of God is wiser than men; and the weakness of God is stronger than men.

I Corinthians 1:18-25

For the proud, it is too much to think that they cannot contribute to their own salvation. Salvation cannot be earned by good works.

For by grace are ye saved through faith;
and that not of yourselves: it is the gift of God:
Not of works, lest any man should boast.

Ephesians 2:8-9

But to those who really know Jesus Christ, the preceding scripture only serves to make their salvation more precious, realizing that their hope is in Christ and Christ alone.

But now in Christ Jesus ye who sometimes were far off are made nigh by the blood of Christ.   Ephesians 2:13

Salvation cannot be purchased by the wealthy. It is free to whosoever will come.

Ho, every one that thirsteth, come ye to the waters, and he that hath no money; come ye, buy, and eat; yea, come,

buy wine and milk without money and without price.
                                              Isaiah 55:1
Forasmuch as ye know that ye were not redeemed with corruptible things, as silver and gold, from your vain conversation received by tradition from your fathers;

But with the precious blood of Christ, as of a lamb without blemish and without spot.   I Peter 1:18, 19

Regardless of a person's position or station in life. salvation is available. Many an individual has had to put aside his talents, or his education, and humble himself realizing that Christ, and Christ alone, could save.

Again we hear from Paul. Paul, the learned; Paul, the religious; Paul, the Pharisee.

Though I might also have confidence in the flesh. If any other man thinketh that he hath whereof he might trust in the flesh, I more:

Circumcised the eighth day, of the stock of Israel, of the tribe of Benjamin, an Hebrew of the Hebrews; as touching the law, a Pharisee;

Concerning zeal, persecuting the church; touching the righteousness which is in the law, blameless.

But what things were gain to me, those I counted loss for Christ.

Yea doubtless, and I count all things but loss for the excellency of the knowledge of Christ Jesus my Lord: for whom I have suffered the loss of all things, and do count them but dung, that I may win Christ,

And be found in him, not having mine own righteousness, which is of the law, but that which is through the faith of Christ, the righteousness which is of God by faith:

That I may know him, and the power of his resurrection, and the fellowship of his sufferings, being made conformable unto his death;

If by any means I might attain unto the resurrection of the dead.   Philippians 3:4-11

Not by works of righteousness which we have done, but according to his mercy he saved us, by the washing of regeneration, and renewing of the Holy Ghost;

Which he shed on us abundantly through Jesus Christ our Saviour;

That being justified by his grace, we should be made heirs according to the hope of eternal life.　　Titus 3:5-7

To the believer, the hope of some day being with Christ, and out of this sinful world, is all important.

Looking for that blessed hope, and the glorious appearing of the great God and our Saviour Jesus Christ.

Titus 2:13

Notice that Paul calls the appearing of Jesus Christ the "blessed hope" of the Christian.

The hope of some day meeting Him — the one who suffered, bled, and died for us and took our place that we could be counted righteous enough to inherit eternal life (II Corinthians 5:21) — is the hope that makes acceptable any suffering a Christian goes through.

Without the hope of someday seeing Christ and being with Him, the Christian life would lose its motivating force.

And if Christ be not raised, your faith is vain; ye are yet in your sins.

Then they also which are fallen asleep in Christ are perished.

If in this life only we have hope in Christ, we are of all men most miserable.　　I Corinthians 15:17-19

Is it enough to be religious? Do all religious paths lead to the same place? Will just being sincere in your beliefs be enough to please God? NO, A THOUSAND TIMES NO!

For God so loved the world, that he gave his only begotten Son, that whosoever believeth in him should not perish, but have everlasting life.

For God sent not his son into the world to condemn the world; but that the world through him might be saved.

He that believeth on him is not condemned: but he that believeth not is condemned already, because he hath not believed in the name of the only begotten Son of God.

John 3:16-18

13

If there is to be a mistake made in any of our doctrine, let it not be in the area of salvation.

Neither is there salvation in any other: for there is none other name under heaven given among men, whereby we must be saved. Acts 4:12

For God hath not appointed us to wrath, but to obtain salvation by our Lord Jesus Christ,

Who died for us, that, whether we wake or sleep, we should live together with him.

Wherefore comfort yourselves together, and edify one another, even as also ye do. I Thessalonians 5:9-11

Therefore we ought to give the more earnest heed to the things which we have heard, lest at any time we should let them slip.

For if the word spoken by angels was stedfast, and every transgression and disobedience received a just recompence of reward;

How shall we escape, if we neglect so great salvation; which at the first began to be spoken by the Lord, and was confirmed unto us by them that heard him.

Hebrews 2:1-3

We need to guard against taking our experience of salvation for granted. Some of the most powerful Christians are those who keep themselves in a constant attitude of thanksgiving for their salvation.

And the seventy returned again with joy, saying, Lord, even the devils are subject unto us through thy name.

And he said unto them, I beheld Satan as lightning fall from heaven.

Behold, I give unto you power to tread on serpents and scorpions, and over all the power of the enemy: and nothing shall by any means hurt you.

Notwithstanding in this rejoice not, that the spirits are subject unto you; but rather rejoice, because your names are written in heaven. Luke 10:17-20

Let us not get so caught up in working for God that we lose our joy and rejoicing over what He has done for us.

Many ministers have become so busy working for God

they forget to tend to their own spiritual condition and they lose out with God.

A few months ago, while ministering in the Philippines, the truth of Luke 10:17-20 was brought before me in a precious way.

I was preaching three times a day in a city-wide crusade at the YMCA gymnasium and the crowds were large. At each evening service, people answered the invitation for salvation in large numbers. Many were filled with the Holy Spirit and some were healed.

After seeing God move in such great outpourings of His Spirit, I would return to my little room where I was staying and the Holy Spirit would come on me so mightily to thank God that my name is written down in heaven, that I would weep for several minutes. I would ask God to never let me see so much that I would grow careless about my own salvation.

As we said before, so say I now again. If any man preach any other gospel unto you than that ye have received, let him be accursed. Galatians 1:9

2
WATER BAPTISM

Several years ago, I was challenged to consider water baptism, its mode and formula, in the following way:

Pretend you have never heard any teaching, from any church or denomination concerning water baptism.

Pretend also that you have been stranded on a deserted island. One day a Bible, protected by a waterproof wrapping, washes up on the island. Remember, you have never been taught on the subject of water baptism. Using only the Bible, what mental pictures would you get of the mode of water baptism?

Would you picture people being sprinkled with a few drops of water, having water poured over them, or being immersed or dipped into the water?

Remember, you are completely untaught and therefore unprejudiced.

Let's look at some scripture passages describing some people being baptized.

Then went out to him Jerusalem, and all Judaea, and all the region round about Jordan,

And were baptized of him in Jordan, confessing their sins.

And Jesus, when he was baptized, went up straightway out of the water: and, lo, the heavens were opened unto him, and he saw the Spirit of God descending like a dove, and lighting upon him. Matthew 3:5, 6, 16

And there went out unto him all the land of Judaea, and they of Jerusalem, and were all baptized of him in the river Jordan, confessing their sins.

And it came to pass in those days, that Jesus came from Nazareth of Galilee, and was baptized of John in Jordan.

And straightway coming up out of the water, he saw the heavens opened, and the Spirit like a dove descending upon Him. Mark 1:5, 9,10

And as they went on their way, they came unto a certain water: and the eunuch said, See, here is water; what doth hinder me to be baptized?

And Philip said, If thou believest with all thine heart, thou mayest. And he answered and said, I believe that Jesus Christ is the Son of God.

And he commanded the chariot to stand still: and they went down both into the water, both Philip and the eunuch; and he baptized him.

And when they were come up out of the water, the Spirit of the Lord caught away Philip, that the eunuch saw him no more; and he went on his way rejoicing.

Acts 8:36-39

Looking at these scriptures, we can readily see that both the one being baptized and the one doing the baptizing went into the water. This certainly would not be necessary if sprinkling were being done, or even pouring.

We see an interesting scripture in the Gospel of John.

And John also was baptizing in Aenon near to Salim, because there was much water there: and they came, and were baptized. John 3:23

If sprinkling were the mode, a pan of water would be sufficient for hundreds; somewhat more would be needed for pouring. **Much** water would be needed for immersion. Notice the scripture said that John was baptizing in this certain place because there was much water.

The words **baptize, baptized,** etc., always come from the Greek word **baptizo,** which means "to make whelmed, to bury or submerge."

Many sincere people have questioned the necessity of total immersion. Why wouldn't sprinkling or pouring be just as effective? The answer, of course, has to do with God's plan, instructions, and types. You see, water baptism is a very important type.

Of what is water baptism a type? Again, on such an important matter, let us consult the Apostle Paul.

Know ye not, that so many of us as were baptized into Jesus Christ were baptized into his death?

17

Therefore we are buried with him by baptism into death: that like as Christ was raised up from the dead by the glory of the Father, even so we also should walk in newness of life.

For if we have been planted together in the likeness of his death, we shall be also in the likeness of his resurrection. Romans 6:3-5

Buried with him in baptism, wherein also ye are risen with him through the faith of the operation of God, who hath raised him from the dead. Colossians 2:12

Baptism is a symbol of death, burial, and resurrection. In fact, it is a symbol that we have died to sin and now the old man is being buried and then we are raised to walk in newness of life. How could you get these symbols from sprinkling or pouring? The obvious answer is that you cannot.

Can you just for a moment imagine taking your deceased loved one to the cemetery, standing the casket upright on the ground, the minister pouring a cupful of dirt over the casket, and then you all leave? When someone asks you what has taken place, you tell them you have just **buried** your deceased loved one. They would think you insane. You cannot bury a person with a few grains or even a cupful of dirt.

Speaking of dirt, I am reminded of the first water baptismal service I ever conducted. A severe drought had affected the area in which I was pastoring. Streams and rivers had become so shallow they were unsuitable for immersing the baptismal candidates. After much searching, we had found a pond on a farm owned by people whose religious denomination taught baptism by sprinkling. (One man called that being dry-cleaned.) They were happy we wanted to use their pond and quickly granted us the permission we desired.

The day of baptizing arrived. The temperature was approximately 100 degrees Fahrenheit. As I led the candidates for baptism out into the middle of the pond, we learned that the mud in the bottom was several inches deep. One dear woman was shaking visibly. Thinking she had taken a chill, I inquired later if she was alright. She then informed me that she was convinced I would lose my grip, drop her in the water, and she would drown.

Please be comforted, I know of no one who has ever been lost in the waters of baptism even though we have baptized in waters which were barely above freezing temperature.

We have baptized the very elderly, some with heart trouble, even some with one or no legs.

To be obedient in following our Lord, Jesus Christ, in water baptism causes there to be a certain sacredness about the service. So often we have felt the presence of God as we have stood in the water.

I remind you again of when John was hesitating to baptize Jesus. When John proceeded, after Jesus urged him, there was a visible and audible approval by God, the Father.

Then cometh Jesus from Galilee to Jordan unto John, to be baptized of him.

But John forbad him, saying, I have need to be baptized of thee, and comest thou to me?

And Jesus answering said unto him, Suffer it to be so now: for thus it becometh us to fulfill all righteousness. Then he suffered him.

And Jesus, when he was baptized, went up straightway out of the water: and, lo, the heavens were opened unto him, and he saw the Spirit of God descending like a dove, and lighting upon him:

And lo a voice from heaven, saying. This is my beloved Son, in whom I am well pleased.   Matthew 3:13-17

Sprinkling or pouring for baptism is the devil's counterfeit of God's plan. They are a substitute for obedience.

Does God care if we do not follow His instructions explicitly?

According to all that I shew thee, after the pattern of the tabernacle, and the pattern of all the *instruments thereof, even so shall ye make it.*

And look that thou make them after their pattern, which was shewed thee in the mount. Exodus 25:9, 40

Who serve unto the example and shadow of heavenly things, as Moses was admonished of God when he was about to make the tabernacle: for, See, saith he, that thou make all things according to the pattern shewed to thee in the mount. Hebrews 8:5

God makes it very clear that He wants His patterns followed.

Is baptism necessary for all believers? Is baptism by immersion necessary to get to heaven?

Go ye therefore, and teach all nations, baptizing them in the name of the Father, and of the Son, and of the Holy Ghost:

Teaching them to observe all things whatsoever I have commanded you: and, lo, I am with you alway, even unto the end of the world. Matthew 28:19, 20

He that believeth and is baptized shall be saved; but he that believeth not shall be damned. Mark 16:16

Can any man forbid water, that these should not be baptized, which have received the Holy Ghost as well as we?

And he commanded them to be baptized in the name of the Lord. Then prayed they him to tarry certain days.

Acts 10:47, 48

Why would someone not want to be baptized? Jesus is our example and pattern. How important did He consider water baptism?

Then cometh Jesus from Galilee to Jordan unto John, to be baptized of him.

But John forbad him, saying, I have need to be baptized of thee, and comest thou to me?

And Jesus answering said unto him, Suffer it to be so now: for thus it becometh us to fulfill all righteousness. Then he suffered him. Matthew 3:13-15

Jesus insisted that John baptize Him in water. Notice then the reaction of the Father.

20

And Jesus, when he was baptized, went up straightway out of the water: and, lo, the heavens were opened unto him, and he saw the Spirit of God descending like a dove, and lighting upon him:

And lo a voice from heaven, saying, This is my beloved Son, in whom I am well pleased.   Matthew 3:16,17

If it was necessary for the Son of God to be baptized in water to fulfill all righteousness and please the Father, then surely it is necessary for us to be baptized.

THE APOSTLE PAUL WAS BAPTIZED:

And Ananias went his way, and entered into the house; and putting his hands on him said, Brother Saul, the Lord, even Jesus, that appeared unto thee in the way as thou camest, hath sent me, that thou mightest receive thy sight, and be filled with the Holy Ghost.

And immediately there fell from his eyes as it had been scales: and he received sight forthwith, and arose, and was baptized.   Acts 9:17,18

Baptism does not free us from sin, the blood of Jesus does this.

But if we walk in the light, as he is in the light, we have fellowship one with another, and the blood of Jesus Christ his Son cleanseth us from all sin.   I John 1:7

Baptism gives us a clear conscience toward God because it is an act of obedience to His command.

The like figure whereunto even baptism doth also now save us (not the putting away of the filth of the flesh, but the answer of a good conscience toward God), by the resurrection of Jesus Christ.   I Peter 3:21

The truly sincere person will obey God and will not try to present foolish arguments against water baptism by referring to the thief on the cross, or putting forth an equally foolish argument that "Uncle Harry was never baptized in water, and if anyone made it to heaven, I know Uncle Harry made it."

What fools we must appear to a Holy God who demands obedience.

If you have never been **baptized by immersion after**

you have been born again, then you need to obey God's Word and be baptized.

It has been my privilege to baptize many who had only been sprinkled.

There are many church groups who are falling into a dangerous precedent. They offer the believer the choice of immersion or sprinkling. This practice reminds me of the man who years ago applied for the position of school teacher in a small community. When asked if he taught whether the world was flat or round, he replied, "I am prepared to teach it either way." And so it is with many religious leaders today. They are prepared to let people have things their own way, without regard to the will and teachings of Almighty God.

To the many who have questioned if they should be immersed again after they have backslidden and went out into sin, and returned to follow the Lord Jesus Christ, I can only answer that if your conscience condemns you it might be well to be re-immersed. Others disagree with me on that and I respect their opinion.

There is no scriptural basis for baptizing infants.

Then Peter said unto them. Repent, and be baptized every one of you in the name of Jesus Christ for the remission of sins, and ye shall receive the gift of the Holy Ghost. Acts 2:38

Several years ago, I became acquainted with a woman who argued strongly for infant baptism. She had begun to attend a Bible class I was teaching and would insist vociferously that her church baptized babies and therefore it must be scripturally correct. Finally, in desperation to prove her belief was correct, she decided to consult her denominational manual, which included the doctrine of infant baptism. Being both an honest and humble person, she sought me out the following day to inform me of her discovery. The chapter on infant baptism began with these words: "There is no place in the Bible where the teaching of infant baptism can be found. We baptize infants solely for the comfort and peace of mind of the infant's parents." At least they were honest.

Baptism follows repentance. I will baptize any infant who will stand and give a clear cut testimony of repentance from his or her sins.

In what name should we be baptized?

Although I deal with this question at length in my discourse on the Trinity, I feel it important to cover it here also.

WHAT IS THE FORMULA BY WHICH WE BAPTIZE?

The answer to this question is extremely important. Many churches, even denominations, have split over the formula of water baptism, or, in other words, what the one doing the baptizing says when baptizing the candidate.

I have always believed Jesus knew what He was doing when he gave us the following instruction:

Go ye therefore, and teach all nations, baptizing them in the name of the Father, and of the Son, and of the Holy Ghost: Matthew 28:19

Lest that should seem simple to you, I tell you again that many churches have been divided over this seemingly simple solution.

Those who believe in baptizing in the name of Jesus, only, argue that Matthew 28:19 does not say in the names of, but rather in the name of.

They also further argue that "Father," "Son," and "Holy Ghost" are not names but titles.

Some dictionaries say that the word **name** is "any word" or "title" by which any person or thing is known.

I call to your attention that this is not just any Father, any Son, or any Holy Ghost, but this is "the Father" of Jesus Christ, and "the Son" of the Father, and "the Holy Ghost," the third person of the Divine Trinity. Any Bible reader should immediately know who those three persons are if mentioned by these names in any scripture.

So many new movements and denominations have been started because some leader has needed his ego flattered. Many individuals, both men and women, have found it necessary to blow some point of doctrine out of proper proportion in order to make sure their followers stayed loyal to them.

In the case of those who insist on water baptism in Jesus' name only, to the extent of waiting outside churches which baptize in the name of the Father, Son, and Holy Ghost, to make proselytes of these followers, it seems to me there must be a wicked spirit involved. I have often wondered if they do this because it is easier than going out and getting their own converts.

Lest this opinion seems cross or bitter, I would ask you to realize that so many of these proselytes are never any good to either group of people any longer. Confusion, hurt, and often bitterness become a way of life to them because of all the wrangling and strife involved.

I would like to share with you a formula for water baptism that I have used for many years.

First, let me say I believe God revealed this to me after much prayer and concern over the number of people making shipwreck of their souls because of the confusion over which name to use when baptizing.

As I am about to immerse the baptismal candidate in water, I first use the person's full name, then add, "upon the profession of your faith, and in the name of Jesus Christ, I now baptize you in the name of the Father, and of the Son, and of the Holy Ghost, amen."

It seems to me, unless a person just wants to be argumentative and divisive, that this formula answers the need. I sympathize with those who want to be baptized in Jesus' name, only. Consider the following scriptures:

Then Peter said unto them, Repent and be baptized every one of you in the name of Jesus Christ for the remission of sins, and ye shall receive the gift of the Holy Ghost.

Acts 2:38

And he commanded them to be baptized in the name of the Lord. Then prayed they him to tarry certain days.

Acts 10:48

When they heard this, they were baptized in the name of

24

the Lord Jesus. Acts 19:5

Now, going back to the formula I shared with you, I believe it covers every objection. You see, it is **in** the **name,** or **authority,** of Jesus Christ that we baptize. And it is **into** the name of the Father, Son, and Holy Ghost we are baptizing.

Let me word it another way. I baptize in the name of the Father, Son, and Holy Ghost, but I am doing this in the name (authority) of Jesus Christ.

We need to realize it is Jesus who told us to baptize. We need to also remember that He told us to baptize in the name of the Father, Son, and Holy Ghost.

Does it seem to you that I am making too big an issue over this? If so, think for just a moment of the peace this has brought to a multitude of believers, both in the U.S.A. and in several other countries.

If someone approaches the believer who has been baptized with this formula and says, "You have not been baptized in the name of Jesus," the baptized person can answer, "Yes, I have been baptized in the name of Jesus."

If someone says, "You have not been baptized in the name of the Father, Son, and Holy Ghost," the baptized person can answer, "Yes, I have been baptized in the name of the Father, Son and Holy Ghost."

In 25 years of baptizing converts, I have never known even one of them to feel their need to be re-baptized.

So, be obedient. Follow Christ in water baptism. If you have only been sprinkled, go the next step, be immersed. And remember, water baptism is not something to quarrel about, it is a beautiful way to identify yourself with Jesus Christ.

As we said before, so say I now again, If any man preach any other gospel unto you than that ye have received, let him be accursed. Galatians 1:9

3
SPEAKING IN TONGUES

There is much confusion about the Holy Spirit baptism.

Multitudes of sincere, God-fearing people claim to have received this experience with the accompanying evidence of speaking in tongues.

What is the baptism of the Holy Spirit? Where does speaking in tongues enter into the picture? Has speaking in tongues ceased?

Before we check with the Apostle Paul on this subject, let's look into several scriptures, forgetting the prejudicial opinions of man.

I indeed baptize you with water unto repentance: but he that cometh after me is mightier than I, whose shoes I am not worthy to bear: he shall baptize you with the Holy Ghost, and with fire: Matthew 3:11

I indeed have baptized you with water: but he shall baptize you with the Holy Ghost.   Mark 1:8

John answered, saying unto them all, I indeed baptize you with water; but one mightier than I cometh, the latchet of whose shoes I am not worthy to unloose: he shall baptize you with the Holy Ghost and with fire:
                    Luke 3:16

And I knew him not: but he that sent me to baptize with water, the same said unto me, Upon whom thou shalt see the Spirit descending, and remaining on him, the same is he which baptizeth with the Holy Ghost.   John 1:33

And, being assembled together with them, commanded them that they should not depart from Jerusalem, but wait for the promise of the Father, which, saith he, ye have heard of me.

For John truly baptized with water; but ye shall be baptized with the Holy Ghost not many days hence.
                    Acts 1:4, 5

Whenever a subject such as this is repeated in the Bible

in five consecutive books, then you can know there is an experience we call the baptism with the Holy Spirit.

It is not the Holy Spirit baptism which is so controversial, rather it is the claim by Pentecostals that speaking in tongues is the initial evidence that a person has received this experience.

Before we examine the evidence, let's determine the purpose.

And, behold, I send the promise of my Father upon you: but tarry ye in the city of Jerusalem, until ye be endued with power from on high. Luke 24:49

But ye shall receive power, after that the Holy Ghost is come upon you: and ye shall be witnesses unto me both in Jerusalem, and in all Judaea, and in Samaria, and unto the uttermost part of the earth. Acts 1:8

The purpose of the infilling of the Holy Spirit is the power to serve God.

Questions must surely arise: Does it make any difference what the initial evidence is? If we do not know what the evidence of receiving is, then how do we know we have received?

Different people make different claims as to how they know they have received.

First, let's look at the account of the great move of God in the city of Samaria.

Then Philip went down to the city of Samaria, and preached Christ unto them.

And the people with one accord gave heed unto those things which Philip spake, hearing and seeing the miracles which he did.

For unclean spirits, crying with loud voice, came out of many that were possessed with them: and many taken with palsies, and that were lame, were healed.

And there was great joy in that city.

But there was a certain man, called Simon, which beforetime in the same city used sorcery, and bewitched the people of Samaria, giving out that himself was some great one:

To whom they all gave heed, from the least to the greatest, saying. This man is the great power of God.

And to him they had regard, because that of long time he had bewitched them with sorceries.

But when they believed Philip preaching the things concerning the kingdom of God, and the name of Jesus Christ, they were baptized, both men and women.

Then Simon himself believed also: and when he was baptized, he continued with Philip, and wondered, beholding the miracles and signs which were done.

Acts 8:5-13

Notice the following events:

1. Christ was preached .... (verse 5).
2. There was unity .... (verse 6).
3. Miracles took place ....(verse 6).
4. Demons were cast out ....(verse 7).
5. Paralyzed people were healed...........(verse 7).
6. Cripples were healed .... (verse 7).
7. People were filled with great joy ......(verse 8).
8. Many were baptized in water...........(verse 12).
9. Signs and miracles were evident ... (verse 13).

What is so amazing is that with all that was happening in Samaria, people had not been baptized with the Holy Spirit.

Now when the apostles which were at Jerusalem heard that Samaria had received the word of God, they sent unto them Peter and John:

Who, when they were come down, prayed for them, that they might receive the Holy Ghost:

(For as yet he was fallen upon none of them: only they were baptized in the name of the Lord Jesus.)

Then laid they their hands on them, and they received the Holy Ghost.

Acts 8:14-17

Notice that when they received the Holy Ghost, something different happened than the nine events before mentioned. We can determine that by the reaction of Simon, the sorcerer. It was when Simon saw the people receiving the Holy Ghost that he offered money to receive the power to do so himself.

And when Simon saw that through laying on of the apostles' hands the Holy Ghost was given, he offered them money,

Saying, Give me also this power, that on whomsoever I lay hands, he may receive the Holy Ghost. Acts 8:18,19

I believe scripture would bear me out that they spoke in tongues. The apostles knew that when people received the Holy Ghost, they spoke with tongues.

While Peter yet spake these words, the Holy Ghost fell on all them which heard the word.

And they of the circumcision which believed were astonished, as many as came with Peter, because that on the Gentiles also was poured out the gift of the Holy Ghost.

For they heard them speak with tongues, and magnify God. Then answered Peter,

Can any man forbid water, that these should not be baptized, which have received the Holy Ghost as well as we?

Acts 10:44-47

Peter knew they had received because, "For they heard them speak with tongues, and magnify God."

In verse 47, Peter states in a question that these received the same way he and the others received on the day of Pentecost.

And when they were come in, they went up into an upper room, where abode both Peter, and James, and John, and Andrew, Philip, and Thomas, Bartholomew, and Matthew, James the son of Alphaeus, and Simon Zeiotes, and Judas the brother of James.

These all continued with one accord in prayer and supplication, with the women, and Mary the mother of Jesus, and with his brethren.

And in those days Peter stood up in the midst of the disciples, and said, (the number of names together were about an hundred and twenty,)

And when the day of Pentecost was fully come, they were all with one accord in one place.

And suddenly there came a sound from heaven as of a rushing mighty wind, and it filled all the house where they were sitting.

And there appeared unto them cloven tongues like as of fire, and it sat upon each of them.

And they were all filled with the Holy Ghost, and began to speak with other tongues, as the Spirit gave them utterance.   Acts 1:13-15; 2:1-4

We find an interesting account in Acts 19:1-6. Here we find the people were not only believers, they had been baptized by immersion in water twice, yet they had not received the Holy Ghost. The same thing happened to them as happened in Acts 2:4 and 10:46.

And it came to pass, that, while Apollos was at Corinth, Paul having passed through the upper coasts came to Ephesus: and finding certain disciples,

He said unto them. Have ye received the Holy Ghost since you believed? And they said unto him. We have not so much as heard whether there be any Holy Ghost.

And he said unto them, Unto what then were ye baptized? And they said, Unto John's baptism.

Then said Paul, John verily baptized with the baptism of repentance, saying unto the people, that they should believe on him which should come after him, that is, on Christ Jesus.

When they heard this, they were baptized in the name of the Lord Jesus.

And when Paul had laid his hands upon them, the Holy Ghost came on them; and they spake with tongues, and prophesied.   Acts 19:1-6

Why is it then that in some Bible accounts tongues was not mentioned when people were filled with the Holy Ghost? It could be because this had become the accepted sign, and the writers did not feel it necessary to mention it every time.

For an example, we can consider that when Paul was filled with the Holy Spirit — a man who was later to become a great apostle — there was no mention of him speaking in tongues.

And Ananias went his way, and entered into the house; and putting his hands on him said, Brother Saul, the Lord, even Jesus, that appeared unto thee in the way as thou earnest, hath sent me, that thou mightest receive thy sight, and be filled with the Holy Ghost.

And immediately there fell from his eyes as it had been scales: and he received sight forthwith, and arose, and was baptized.

And when he had received meat, he was strengthened. Then was Saul certain days with the disciples which were at Damascus. Acts 9:17-19

Again I ask, could it be that since tongues were the accepted sign the writer felt no compelling need to mention them? I say this without timidity because we know the Apostle Paul spoke with tongues.

Let us look to him for the proof:

I thank my God, I speak with tongues more than ye all:

Yet in the church I had rather speak five words with my understanding, that by my voice I might teach others also, than ten thousand words in an unknown tongue.

I Corinthians 14:18,19

Why speak in tongues at all? What profit is there in speaking in a language we cannot understand?

Many people think Paul was able to make the claim of speaking in tongues more than his fellows because he was well educated and knew several languages. However, there is a serious mistake in this belief. Speaking in tongues is a supernatural language one receives when he is baptized with the Holy Spirit. If a person could speak in tongues because he knew another language, then anyone could speak in tongues whether or not he received the Holy Ghost, simply by learning another language.

To the spiritually unlearned, speaking in tongues is useless if not foolish. To the child of God who prays regularly in tongues, speaking in tongues holds a very great place in his life. Why?

31

Follow after charity, and desire spiritual gifts, but rather that ye may prophesy.

For he that speaketh in an unknown tongue speaketh not unto men, but unto God: for no man understandeth him; how-beit in the spirit he speaketh mysteries.

But he that prophesieth speaketh unto men to edification, and exhortation and comfort.

He that speaketh in an unknown tongue edifieth himself; but he that prophesieth edifieth the church.

I Corinthians 14:1-4

Speaking in tongues edifies, or builds up, the one doing the speaking. Do Christians need to build themselves up?

But ye, beloved building up yourselves on your most holy faith, praying in the Holy Ghost,   Jude 20

The command is to pray in the Holy Ghost and build ourselves up. Why?

Keep yourselves in the love of God, looking for the mercy of our Lord Jesus Christ unto eternal life.   Jude 21

Now if Paul spoke in tongues more than the rest, and thus could build himself up more than the rest because he knew several languages, why would he say the following?

For if I pray in an unknown tongue, my spirit prayeth, but my understanding is unfruitful.

What is it then? I will pray with the spirit, and I will pray with the understanding also: I will sing with the spirit, and I will sing with the understanding also.

I Corinthians 14:14, 15

Speaking in tongues, or praying in tongues, is praying with the Spirit, or as Jude says, "Praying in the Holy Ghost," the purpose of which is to build yourself up to become a better servant of God.

Paul who claimed to "speak with tongues more than ye all," is also considered the greatest apostle. Also, he stated that, "Yet in the church I had rather speak five words with my understanding..." Where did he do all this speaking in tongues? The answer is obvious. He did it in his private prayer life. That is where he built himself up, to build up

God's kingdom.

Let it be said here that there are those who make much of speaking in tongues who are very carnal. Many were like that in the church at Corinth. This seems to be the compelling reason for I Corinthians 13. Speaking in tongues alone will not make you spiritual. Speaking in tongues while living in harmony with all of God's revealed will is of great value.

Charity never faileth: but whether there be prophecies, they shall fail; whether there be tongues, they shall cease; whether there be knowledge, it shall vanish away.

For we know in part, and we prophesy in part.

But when that which is perfect is come, then that which is in part shall be done away.   I Corinthians 13:8-10

Some would say, referring to I Corinthians 13:8-10, that speaking in tongues has ceased and is not for today. They say, "that which is perfect" refers to the Bible. They ignore the next two verses which fully explain that Paul is talking about the next life, the completeness and perfection of our glorified lives with Christ. In fact, many of these same people use this scripture to prove we will know our loved ones in heaven.

The Apostle Peter helps us to understand that the promise of the Holy Ghost was not just for those in Bible days.

Then Peter said unto them, Repent, and be baptized every one of you in the name of Jesus Christ for the remission of sins, and ye shall receive the gift of the Holy Ghost.

For the promise is unto you, and to your children, and to all that are afar off, even as many as the Lord our God shall call.   Acts 2:38, 39

Some have tried to prove that speaking in other tongues is not of God because women speak in tongues, sometimes in the church.

Let your women keep silence in the churches: for it is not permitted unto them to speak; but they are commanded to be under obedience, as also saith the law.

And if they will learn anything, let them ask their hus-

bands at home: for it is a shame for women to speak in the
church. I Corinthians 14:34, 35

The preceding scripture plainly says, "if they will learn anything ..." and has nothing to do with speaking in tongues, prophesying, or testifying. I have attended several churches where this argument is used, yet their women testify, teach Sunday School classes, and even stand on the platform to lead the singing.

The scripture plainly teaches that the baptism of the Holy Ghost with speaking in other tongues is for women as well as men.

And it shall come to pass afterward, that I will pour out my spirit upon all flesh; and your sons and your daughters shall prophesy, your old men shall dream dreams, your young men shall see visions:

And also upon the servants and upon the handmaids in those days will I pour out my spirit. Joel 2:28, 29

These all continued with one accord in prayer and supplication, with the women, and Mary the mother of Jesus, and with his brethren. Acts 1:14

And it shall come to pass in the last days, saith God, I will pour out of my Spirit upon all flesh: and your sons and your daughters shall prophesy, and your young men shall see visions, and your old men shall dream dreams:

And on my servants and on my handmaidens I will pour out in those days of my Spirit; and they shall prophesy.
Acts 2:17, 18

Speaking in tongues is the privilege of every Spirit-filled believer. It must be understood that **every** Spirit-filled believer can pray, sing, and worship God in other tongues.

This heavenly language is given to the believer upon receiving their personal Holy Spirit baptism and can be used at will.

However, not everyone has the **gift** of bringing a message in tongues in the church to be interpreted. To bring a message in tongues, one must have the gift of tongues and not just the evidence of tongues. Also, this gift cannot be

34

used at will, but must be activated by the anointing of the Holy Spirit.

Paul was talking about the gift of tongues when he wrote:

Have all the gifts of healing? do all speak with tongues? do all interpret?   I Corinthians 12:30

I will speak more of the **gift** of tongues in another chapter.

As we said before, so say I now again, If any man preach any other gospel unto you that ye have received, let him be accursed.   Galatians 1:9

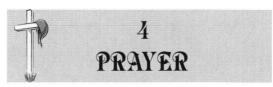

4
PRAYER

Praying always with all prayer and supplication in the Spirit, and watching thereunto with all perseverance and supplication for all saints;　　　　Ephesians 6:18

There can be no doubt, that of all praying people, Jesus was the master pray-er.

Many people have read "The Lord's Prayer" without recognizing the power and depth contained therein.

When we realize that Jesus was teaching as the rabbis of that day taught, by listing certain topics and then under that topic providing a complete outline, we realize we have come upon great truth.

In this model prayer we now know as "The Lord's Prayer," Jesus enumerated topics and instructed, "After this manner therefore pray ye:" (Matthew 6:9)

And he said unto them, When ye pray, say.　　　Luke 11:2

Is it not amazing, then, that when most people pray they say anything and everything but what the Lord told them to say?

We memorize the Lord's prayer, we quote it, we sing it, but few pray it, using the Lord's prayer as a group of six topics, under the guidance of the Holy Spirit.

Allow me to list these six topics:

(1) Our Father which art in heaven, Hallowed be thy name.

(2) Thy kingdom come. Thy will be done.

(3) Give us this day our daily bread.

(4) Forgive us our debts (sins) as we forgive our debtors.

(5) And lead us not into temptation, but deliver us from evil.

(6) For thine is the kingdom, and the power, and the glory, forever.

If we will take each of these topics before the Lord, patiently, carefully, we will find it difficult to not spend at least one hour in prayer each day.

And he cometh unto the disciples, and findeth them asleep, and saith unto Peter, What, could ye not watch with me one hour? Matthew 26:40

Could it be that Jesus is asking that same question of the church today?

Someone has said prayer is the most talked about, least practiced subject in the church today.

If it is true the church goes forward on its knees, could it be that the church is almost standing still?

And he spake a parable unto them to this end, that men ought always to pray, and not to faint; Luke 18:1

Along with our Lord Jesus Christ, I find it extremely interesting to listen in on the prayers of the Apostle Paul. Here's a man who knows how to pray.

I will therefore that men pray every where, lifting up holy hands, without wrath and doubting. I Timothy 2:8

Wherefore also we pray always for you, that our God would count you worthy of this calling, and fulfill all the good pleasure of his goodness, and the work of faith with power:

That the name of our Lord Jesus Christ may be glorified in you, and ye in him according to the grace of our God and the Lord Jesus Christ. II Thessalonians 1:11, 12

It seems Paul continually prayed for his converts. It appears he prayed more for saints than for sinners.

First, I thank my God through Jesus Christ for you all, that your faith is spoken of throughout the whole world.

For God is my witness, whom I serve with my spirit in the gospel of his Son, that without ceasing I make mention of you always in my prayers; Romans 1:8, 9

I thank my God always on your behalf, for the grace of God which is given you by Jesus Christ; I Corinthians 1:4

Wherefore I also, after I heard of your faith in the Lord Jesus, and love unto all the saints,

Cease not to give thanks for you, making mention of you in my prayers; Ephesians 1:15,16

I thank my God upon every remembrance of you,

Always in every prayer of mine for you all making request with joy,

For your fellowship in the gospel from the first day until now;   Philippians 1:3-5

We give thanks to God and the Father of our Lord Jesus Christ, praying always for you,   Colossians 1:3

We give thanks to God always for you all, making mention of you in our prayers;

Remembering without ceasing your work of faith, and labour of love, and patience of hope in our Lord Jesus Christ, in the sight of God and our Father;

I Thessalonians 1:2, 3

We are bound to thank God always for you, brethren, as it is meet, because that your faith groweth exceedingly, and the charity of every one of you all toward each other aboundeth;   II Thessalonians 1:3

Could it be that Paul was such a great man in the pulpit because he was such a great man in the prayer closet?

I have long been intrigued by Paul's personal statement concerning speaking with tongues.

I thank my God, I speak with tongues more than ye all:

Yet in the church I had rather speak five words with my understanding, that by my voice I might teach others also, than ten thousand words in an unknown tongue.

I Corinthians 14:18, 19

What is it then? I will pray with the spirit, and I will pray with the understanding also:

I will sing with the spirit, and I will sing with the understanding also.   I Corinthians 14:15

He that speaketh in an unknown tongue edifieth himself; but he that prophesieth edifieth the church.

I Corinthians 14:4

Paul evidently spent much time building himself up by praying. Lest that sound selfish or carnal, we need to realize we cannot give to someone else something we ourselves do not possess.

If Christians ever come to realize the power of prayer, it

may be difficult to get them to do much else.

In Paul's epistle to the church at Ephesus, we can glimpse a little of the potential of increased wisdom and revelation through prayer.

Wherefore I also, after I heard of your faith in the Lord Jesus, and love unto all the saints,

Cease not to give thanks for you, making mention of you in my prayers;

That the God of our Lord Jesus Christ, the Father of glory, may give unto you the spirit of wisdom and revelation in the knowledge of him:

The eyes of your understanding being enlightened; that ye may know what is the hope of his calling, and what the riches of the glory of his inheritance in the saints,

And what is the exceeding greatness of his power to usward who believe, according to the working of his mighty power,

Which he wrought in Christ, when he raised him from the dead, and set him at his own right hand in the heavenly places,

Far above all principality, and power, and might, and dominion, and every name that is named, not only in this world, but also in that which is to come:

And hath put all things under his feet, and gave him to be the head over all things to the church,

Which is his body, the fulness of him that filleth all in all. Ephesians 1:15-23

It would be well for us to pray that prayer, putting ourselves, or even our own name in the prayer.

We travel a little further on in Ephesians and find Paul praying again for the Christians.

For this cause I bow my knees unto the Father of our Lord Jesus Christ,

Of whom the whole family in heaven and earth is named,

That he would grant you, according to the riches of his glory, to be strengthened with might by his Spirit in the inner man;

That Christ may dwell in your hearts by faith; that ye, being rooted and grounded in love,

May be able to comprehend with all saints what is the breadth, and length, and depth, and height;

And to know the love of Christ, which passeth knowledge, that ye might be filled with all the fulness of God.

Now unto him that is able to do exceeding abundantly above all that we ask or think, according to the power that worketh in us,

Unto him be glory in the church by Christ Jesus throughout all ages, world without end. Amen.

Ephesians 3:14-21

Paul doesn't stop praying for the Christians, he instructs us to do the same.

Praying always with all prayer and supplication in the Spirit, and watching thereunto with all perseverance and supplication for all saints; Ephesians 6:18

In his discourse on the armor of God, most of us have missed the weapon of prayer. We have mistakenly ended with ".. . the helmet of salvation, and the sword of the Spirit, which is the word of God."

We need to go on to verse 18 and include one of the greatest weapons in the Christians' arsenal, the weapon of prayer.

I believe prayer is one of the mighty weapons Paul referred to when talking about pulling down strongholds.

For though we walk in the flesh, we do not war after the flesh:

(For the weapons of our warfare are not carnal, but mighty through God to the pulling down of strong holds;)

Casting down imaginations, and every high thing that exalteth itself against the knowledge of God, and bringing into captivity every thought to the obedience of Christ; II Corinthians 10:3-5

Jesus also taught about this matter of pulling down

strongholds.

And others, tempting him, sought of him a sign from heaven.

But he, knowing their thoughts, said unto them, Every kingdom divided against itself is brought to desolation; and a house divided against a house falleth.

If Satan also be divided against himself, how shall his kingdom stand? because ye say that I cast out devils through Beelzebub.

And if I by Beelzebub cast out devils, by whom do your sons cast them out? therefore shall they be your judges.

But if I with the finger of God cast out devils, no doubt the kingdom of God is come upon you.

When a strong man armed keepeth his palace, his goods are in peace:

But when a stronger than he shall come upon him, and overcome him, he taketh from him all his armour wherein he trusted, and divided his spoils.   Luke 11:16-22

The "strong man armed" in verse 21 is the devil. The "stronger than he" in verse 22 can be us, you and me.

One of the greatest weapons we can use against the "strong man" is the weapon of prayer.

Prayer, combined with fasting, is even more powerful. Daniel is a prime example.

Now when Daniel knew that the writing was signed, he went into his house; and his windows being open in his chamber toward Jerusalem, he kneeled upon his knees three times a day, and prayed, and gave thanks before his God, as he did aforetime.   Daniel 6:1

In those days I Daniel was mourning three full weeks.

I ate no pleasant bread, neither came flesh nor wine in my mouth, neither did I anoint myself at all, till three whole weeks were fulfilled.

Then said he unto me, Fear not, Daniel: for from the first day that thou didst set thine heart to understand, and to chasten thyself before thy God, thy words were heard, and I am come for thy words.   Daniel 10:2, 3,12

We have many biblical examples of men who prayed, and many who prayed and fasted. Yes, prayer is hard work. No doubt that is why so few **really** pray.

However, there is a prayer that brings refreshment from God.

He giveth power to the faint; and to them that have no might he increaseth strength.

Even the youths shall faint and be weary, and the young men shall utterly fall:

But they that wait upon the Lord shall renew their strength; they shall mount up with wings as eagles; they shall run, and not be weary; and they shall walk, and not faint.   Isaiah 40:29-31

There is a prayer that contends with God for a definite answer.

Produce your cause, saith the Lord; bring forth your strong reasons, saith the King of Jacob.   Isaiah 41:21

There are times when God wants us to contend with Him. Times when the Holy Spirit will anoint us to pray fearful prayers.

Years ago, when we were in the beginning stages of the work in Independence, Iowa, we had a need of $300. Now this may not seem like much to you, but back then it seemed a huge amount. With only a handful of people, and the average Sunday evening offering less than $5.00, I went to prayer on Sunday afternoon. What started out to be a nice, quiet, mild request, became very fervent. I prayed something like this, "God, we have to have $300 by tomorrow morning. You said you would 'supply all my needs according to your riches in glory by Christ Jesus.' God, if you don't supply this money by tomorrow morning, you are a liar." There it was. It was out before I knew it. Immediately I asked God to forgive me, but a strange thing happened. The Holy Spirit began to talk to my heart. He said, "Do not be afraid, that was not you, I was anointing you to pray like that."

Likewise the Spirit also helpeth our infirmities: for we know not what we should pray for as we ought: but the

Spirit itself maketh intercession for us with groanings which cannot be uttered.

And he that searcheth the hearts knoweth what is the mind of the Spirit, because he maketh intercession for the saints according to the will of God.

And we know that all things work together for good to them that love God, to them who are the called according to his purpose. Romans 8:26-28

But then, in the Sunday evening service, I made a grave mistake. In the excitement of God's blessing, I forgot to ask for the $300. Alas, alas.

"Oh well," I thought, "we never get more than $5.00 in the evening service anyway."

As I was standing at the door to shake hands after the service, a lady visitor shook my hand and pressed into it a piece of paper. I calmly put it in my pocket, thinking it was a check for $5.00 or at the most $20.00. Later, when I looked, I saw it was made out for $350.00.

Again, the Holy Spirit spoke to my heart. He said, "God gave you $50.00 more than you asked for so you would know He is not a cheapskate."

Yes, what would happen if we would learn to pray like Jesus, and Paul?

As we said before, so say I now again, If any man preach any other gospel unto you than that ye have received, let him be accursed. Galatians 1:9

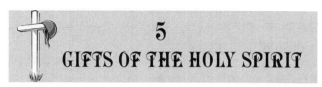

5
GIFTS OF THE HOLY SPIRIT

Now concerning spiritual gifts, brethren, I would not have you ignorant.   I Corinthians 12:1

Someone has remarked, that of all the teachings in the Bible we are **ignorant** of, we are **more** ignorant of the teaching of the gifts of the Spirit than **any** other. And this after Paul says "... I would not have you ignorant."

On this subject, as well as so many others, we look for enlightenment to the Apostle Paul. In fact, it seems the Apostle Paul, and he only, has been singled out by the Holy Spirit to bring in-depth teaching concerning these miraculous gifts.

Because of lack of understanding, many have ignored, or shied away from the gifts of the Spirit. Others have mistakenly pushed aside these supernatural gifts and relegated them to bygone days. Some have said these gifts are no longer needed and have ceased to be in operation since the days of the apostles.

Let's look at several aspects of these gifts. For instance:

THE NEED FOR THE GIFTS TODAY
WHAT IS THE PURPOSE OF THE GIFTS?
HOW MANY GIFTS ARE THERE?
WHOSE GIFTS ARE THEY?
TO WHOM ARE THE GIFTS GIVEN?
WHAT ABOUT THE LOVE FACTOR?

THE NEED FOR THE GIFTS TODAY:

Can any deny the desperate need of the church today in its effort to reach out to a degenerate world?

Some would argue that the gifts were given to prove God's Word to be true and establish the church in the early days, the beginning of Christianity. I cannot disagree with this premise; however, do we not still need them for the very same purpose?

Surely, the church today needs credibility in a perverted

world. Surely all the scoffers and skeptics did not pass with the days of the apostles.

The devil is still loose. The manifesting of the work of demon powers is seen on every hand.

Each child of God needs the gifts in order to be able to cope with satanic powers and defeat the works of the devil in the lives of men.

WHAT IS THE PURPOSE OF THE GIFTS?

But the manifestation of the Spirit is given to every man to profit withal.   I Corinthians 12:7

Follow after charity, and desire spiritual gifts, but rather that ye may prophesy.

For he that speaketh in an unknown tongue speaketh not unto men, but unto God: for no man understandeth him; howbeit in the spirit he speaketh mysteries.

I Corinthians 14:1, 2

In a nutshell, the purpose of the gifts is the **edifying** of the church. Paul makes this clear in his discourse concerning tongues and interpretation of tongues.

Follow after charity, and desire spiritual gifts, but rather that ye may prophesy.

For he that speaketh in an unknown tongue speaketh not unto men, but unto God: for no man understandeth him; howbeit in the spirit he speaketh mysteries.

But he that prophesieth speaketh unto men to edification, and exhortation, and comfort.

He that speaketh in an unknown tongue edifieth himself; but he that prophesieth edifieth the church.

I would that ye all spake with tongues, but rather that ye prophesied: for greater is he that prophesieth than he that speaketh with tongues, except he interpret, that the church may receive edifying.   I Corinthians 14:1-5

". . . that the church may receive edifying" is the crux of the matter.

Christ loves His church, make no mistake about it, this is His body.

So we, being many, are one body in Christ, and every one members one of another.   Romans 12:5

For we being many are one bread, and one body: for we are all partakers of that one bread. I Corinthians 10:17

For as the body is one, and hath many members, and all the members of that one body, being many, are one body: so also is Christ I Corinthians 12:12

Which he wrought in Christ, when he raised him from the dead, and set him at his own right hand in the heavenly places,

Far above all principality, and power, and might, and dominion, and every name that is named, not only in this world, but also in that which is to come:

And hath put all things under his feet, and gave him to be the head over all things to the church,

Which is his body, the fulness of him that filleth all in all. Ephesians 1:20-23

And he is the head of the body, the church: who is the beginning, the firstborn from the dead; that in all things he might have the preeminence. Colossians 1:18

Again, in the discourse concerning tongues and prophecy, Paul emphasizes it is more important to edify or build up the whole church, rather than just one individual. He goes on to explain that tongues with the interpretation is equal to prophecy.

I would that ye all spake with tongues, but rather that ye prophesied: for greater is he that prophesieth than he that speaketh with tongues, except he interpret, that the church may receive edifying. I Corinthians 14:5

HOW MANY GIFTS ARE THERE?

For to one is given by the Spirit the word of wisdom; to another the word of knowledge by the same Spirit;

To another faith by the same Spirit; to another the gifts of healing by the same Spirit;

To another the working of miracles; to another prophecy; to another discerning of spirits; to another divers kinds of tongues; to another the interpretation of tongues: I Corinthians 12:8-10

1. The gift of the word of wisdom.

46

2. The gift of the word of knowledge.
3. The gift of faith.
4. The gifts of healing.
5. The gift of the working of miracles.
6. The gift of prophecy.
7. The gift of discerning of spirits.
8. The gift of divers kinds of tongues.
9. The gift of interpretation of tongues.

Although I have listed the number and names of the gifts, allow me to put them into three classifications, or categories, so they may be identified more easily.

I. THE REVELATION GIFTS

1. The gift of the word of wisdom.
2. The gift of the word of knowledge.
3. The gift of discerning of spirits.

II. THE POWER GIFTS

1. The gift of faith.
2. The gifts of healing.
3. The gift of the working of miracles.

III. THE VOCAL GIFTS

1. The gift of divers kinds of tongues.
2. The gift of interpretation of tongues.
3. The gift of prophecy.

It may be easier for you to remember the nine gifts in these three categories.

WHOSE GIFTS ARE THEY?

Now there are diversities of gifts, but the same Spirit.

And there are differences of administrations, but the same Lord.

And there are diversities of operations, but it is the same God which worketh all in all.

But the manifestation of the Spirit is given to every man to profit withal.   I Corinthians 12:4-7

Without a doubt, the gifts belong to the Holy Spirit. Therefore, they are His to give.

*For to one is **given by the Spirit** the word of wisdom; to another the word of knowledge **by the same Spirit;***

*To another faith **by the same Spirit;** to another the gifts of healing **by the same Spirit;*** I Corinthians 12:8, 9

TO WHOM ARE THE GIFTS GIVEN?

But all these worketh that one and the selfsame Spirit, dividing to every man severally as he will.

I Corinthians 12:11

I find the preceding scripture to be good news indeed. While it is true the Spirit gives the gifts according to His will, the verse also says "... dividing to every man." It seems obvious, at least to me, that any and every born again, Spirit filled believer is a likely candidate to receive one or more gifts of the Holy Spirit. Notice the word "severally" in verse 11. I call special attention to that word as it is very important.

There are those who teach that every Spirit filled believer has all nine gifts of the Holy Spirit in him, potentially at least. They teach one person can have all nine gifts of the Spirit in actual experience and usage. Others teach that a Spirit filled believer can have only one or two gifts.

So now, let's look at that word "severally." Does it mean that the Spirit gives **several** gifts to every man? That is **not** the meaning. The word "severally" is from the Greek word **idios** which means private, or separate, alone, apart, aside, their own.

This is very interesting, especially the word **alone.** Does this mean one gift **alone?** No, that is not the meaning. The word **severally** does not mean **one alone** or **many.** It simply means the gifts are the property of the Holy Spirit, to be given at His will, to whomever He pleases. He will give these gifts as He chooses, privately, separately, alone, apart and aside from what anyone else thinks, feels, or says about it. It will be Him, alone, dealing with each individual, alone, without consideration to what, if any gifts, someone else may have. If the Spirit wants to give one gift or nine gifts to an individual, that is between the giver and the receiver of the gift, or gifts, alone.

Can the Holy Spirit be influenced by the receiver? I believe He can and will be influenced by the individual whose heart is hungry to serve and glorify God with the gift(s).

Blessed are they which do hunger and thirst after righteousness: for they shall be filled.   Matthew 5:6

But covet earnestly the best gifts: and yet shew I unto you a more excellent way.   I Corinthians 12:31

Follow after charity, and desire spiritual gifts ...   I Corinthians 14:1

I cannot believe God wants us to hunger and thirst, covet and desire, if He did not intend to answer. So, therefore, any member of the body, Christ's body, who hungers and thirsts for, or covets and desires after, the gifts of the Holy Spirit is a likely candidate to receive.

WHAT ABOUT THE LOVE FACTOR?

There are those who really get confused at this point. I have heard speakers say the gifts of the Spirit are not important, it's love that counts. Others have thought that I Corinthians 13 was a misplaced chapter. Not at all! Look and see and marvel at the wisdom of God when He moves upon His servant Paul.

God knew there would be those who would receive a **gift,** then get puffed up with pride because of that gift. He knew others would try to use their **gift** to usurp authority or **lord** it over someone who did not have a gift.

So God straightens it all out in the thirteenth chapter.

Though I speak with the tongues of men and of angels, and have not charity, I am become as sounding brass, or a tinkling cymbal.

And though l have the gift of prophecy, and understand all mysteries, and all knowledge; and though I have all faith, so that I could remove mountains, and have not charity, I am nothing.

And though I bestow all my goods to feed the poor, and though I give my body to be burned, and have not charity, I am nothing.   I Corinthians 13:1-3

"Look," God is saying, "You can have the gift of prophecy, the gift of discerning of spirits, the gift of the word of knowledge, and the gift of faith, but, if these gifts are not controlled and regulated by love, and that love is not found in you, you are **nothing."** Notice, He didn't say you are **lacking somewhat.** He didn't say you were a **little** less **than the** best. He says, "Nothing," zero, zilch.

He goes on to say:

Charity suffereth long, and is kind; charity envieth not; charity vaunteth not itself, is not puffed up.

Doth not behave itself unseemly, seeketh not her own, is not easily provoked, thinketh no evil;

Rejoiceth not in iniquity, but rejoiceth in the truth;

Beareth all things, believeth all things, hopeth all things, endureth all things. I Corinthians 13:4-7

Charity, which is taken from the Greek word **agape,** means the highest form of love. This love will keep us from being proud, harsh, and impatient with others. Man has a problem. When he feels spiritual, or used of God, he begins to get proud or impatient with those he feels to be less spiritual. Agape love takes care of that problem.

Should we then seek to excel in love and neglect the spiritual gifts? No, this is not God's will at all. Watch this:

But covet earnestly the best gifts: and yet shew I unto you a more excellent way. I Corinthians 12:31

And now abideth faith, hope, charity, these three; but the greatest of these is charity. I Corinthians 13:13

Follow after charity, and desire spiritual gifts, but rather that ye may prophesy. I Corinthians 14:1

The answer is to follow after agape love **and** desire spiritual gifts. How can any sincere believer miss this obvious answer unless he has been prejudiced by prior teaching?

Paul closes out Chapter 12 by saying, "I shew unto you a more excellent way." Then he spends an entire chapter, Chapter 13, talking about love. And then he tells us in so many words, "Go for it, get it all!"

To those who say the gifts have ceased with the passing of the New Testament apostles, let me point out that the words in verses 10 through 12 are talking about heaven, not the passing of the apostles, or the printing of the Bible.

Charity never faileth: but whether there be prophecies, they shall fail; whether there be tongues, they shall cease; whether there be knowledge, it shall vanish away.

For we know in part, and we prophesy in part.

But when that which is perfect is come, then that which is in part shall be done away.   I Corinthians 13:8-10

Paul is clearly referring here to our limited state of knowledge in this present world as compared to what we will know in heaven. Remember, the gift of the "**word** of knowledge" is not, as some mistakenly believe, the gift of knowledge. Even with the gifts we are severely limited compared to how we will know in heaven. When Paul says, "...then shall I know even as also I am known," he is clearly referring to heaven and our glorified bodies.

Allow me to give a brief description of each of the gifts and their individual functions in edifying the body of Christ.

I. THE REVELATION GIFTS

1. THE GIFT OF THE WORD OF WISDOM

The gift of the word of wisdom is a **supernatural** revelation of one tiny part of God's wisdom to the recipient of this gift. It is **miraculous** as all the gifts are.

It is **not** natural wisdom, psychology, or human insight.

2. THE GIFT OF THE WORD OF KNOWLEDGE

The gift of the word of knowledge is a **supernatural** revelation of one bit or particle of God's tremendous storehouse of knowledge.

It is **not** suspicion, worry, or guessing. It **does not** have anything to do with what we studied in school, it is **not** human intellect.

3. THE GIFT OF DISCERNING OF SPIRITS.

The gift of discerning of spirits is the **supernatural** ability to look into the realm of the spirit world, at least enough to know whether a spirit is good or bad.

It is **not** fortune telling, seances, or witchcraft.

II. POWER GIFTS
1. THE GIFT OF FAITH.
The gift of faith is the **supernatural** ability to believe what God says is an established fact. It is God's faith **miraculously** placed in our heart,

It is **not** mind over matter, emotion, or just hoping.
2. THE GIFTS OF HEALING.
The gifts of healing is the **supernatural** ability to impart divine healing effecting deliverance from pain, sickness, and disease. It is **not** medical science or psychology.
3. THE GIFT OF THE WORKING OF MIRACLES.
The gift of the working of miracles is the **supernatural** ability to intervene in the course of nature when the work of God can be furthered. I believe some healings can really be attributed to the working of miracles in conjunction with the gifts of healing.

III. THE VOCAL GIFTS
1. THE GIFT OF TONGUES.
The gift of diverse kinds of tongues is the **supernatural** ability to deliver a message in a language unknown to the speaker.

It is **not** the ability to learn and speak foreign languages.

I believe it is different from the evidence of tongues given when a person is baptized with the Holy Ghost.
2. THE GIFT OF INTERPRETATION OF TONGUES.
The gift of the interpretation of tongues is the **supernatural** ability to interpret or make clear what has been spoken in another tongue.

It is **not** knowing the language which has just been spoken. It is **not** guessing at what you **think** the message was meant to be.
3. THE GIFT OF PROPHECY.
The gift of prophecy is the **supernatural** ability to speak a message direct from God in your own, known language.

It is **not** anointed preaching. It is not giving someone a "piece of your mind" in religious disguise.

I do believe anointed preaching sometimes merges with prophecy when the preacher proclaims anointed truths that he himself was unaware of until God revealed it to him at that moment.

May I point out to you that when any of these gifts are operating, the person using the gifts still has control of himself? Some have done outlandish things claiming they were **forced** by the Holy Spirit.

And the spirits of the prophets are subject to the prophets.

For God is not the author of confusion, but of peace, as in all churches of the saints.   I Corinthians 14:32, 33

I think it would be well to let the Apostle Paul close this chapter.

Let all things be done decently and in order.

I Corinthians 14:40

As we said before, so say I now again. If any man preach any other gospel unto you than that ye have received, let him be accursed.   Galatians 1:9

6
TITHING

What about this matter of tithing? Why are there so many different views by so many different individuals and churches?

Isn't it true that tithing was instituted under the law of Moses, and the entire New Testament is silent on this subject?

And if a person is supposed to tithe, where and when would he pay or give that tithe, and how much should it be?

I will attempt, with God's Word and God's help, to answer all of these questions.

First, let me say, I am a firm believer in tithing. But then, after all, I am a pastor. Being a pastor supported by money from the tithes of Christians, I would be somewhat stupid to not believe in tithing.

And then, let me say, that it really does not make any difference what I believe, or you believe, or any group or denomination believes, if that belief is not scripturally correct.

We will probably wait until about the end of this chapter to see what, if anything, the Apostle Paul has to say about this matter. For now, let's do some research on tithing.

And all the tithe of the land, whether of the seed of the land, or of the fruit of the tree, is the Lord's: it is holy unto the Lord.

And if a man will at all redeem ought of his tithes, he shall add thereto the fifth part thereof.

And concerning the tithe of the herd, or of the flock, even of whatsoever passeth under the rod, the tenth shall be holy unto the Lord.

He shall not search whether it be good or bad, neither shall he change it: and if he change it at all, then both it and the change thereof shall be holy: it shall not be re-

deemed.

*These are the commandments, which the Lord command-
ed Moses for the children of Israel in Mount Sinai.*

Leviticus 27:30-34

It doesn't take us long to run across the doctrine of tithing in the Old Testament.

We see in the preceding scriptures that the tithe belonged to the Lord, and was considered to be holy.

If you care to do your own checking on the word **tithe,**
you will promptly discover that tithe means tenth.

So, God was saying that a tenth of land, seed, fruit of the
tree, the herd, the flock, etc., belonged to God. In fact, He
just makes it outright plain, "It is the Lord's."

The scripture goes on to say in this instance if you hold
back your tithe, or borrow it, you must pay twenty percent
on the ten percent. Sounds like a stiff penalty to me.

That tithing was commanded under the law of Moses can
hardly be denied. In addition to Leviticus 27:30-34, we
have a startling question, accusation, and commandment
from God in Malachi 3:8-10.

*Will a man rob God? Yet ye have robbed me. But ye say,
Wherein have we robbed thee? In tithes and offerings.*

*Ye are cursed with a curse: for ye have robbed me, even
this whole nation.*

*Bring ye all the tithes into the storehouse, that there may
be meat in mine house, and prove me now herewith, saith
the Lord of hosts, if I will not open you the windows of
heaven, and pour you out a blessing, that there shall not
be room enough to receive it.* Malachi 3:8-10

Here we have God establishing the truth that to not pay
God the tithe is to be a robber, crook, or thief. He also
plainly states there is a curse pronounced on the non-
tither.

You will probably notice I usually refer to tithes being
paid rather than given. The reason for this is easily seen if
you take into account the truth given in Leviticus 27:30-
34 and Malachi 3:8-10. How can you give someone some-

55

thing that is already his? Also, if you are considered a robber for not bringing in all the tithes, then you certainly could not be considered to be giving a gift if you do bring them in.

I would not go to the electric company, hand them some money along with my bill, and tell them I had come to give them a gift. No, I was only paying them what was due them. So it is with the tithes.

We know that tithing was commanded under the law of Moses, but tithing did not originate there. It seems tithing has always been required by God.

The first recorded instance of tithe being paid was by Abram to Melchizedek approximately 430 years before the law of Moses was given.

And Melchizedek king of Salem brought forth bread and wine: and he was the priest of the most high God.

And he blessed him, and said. Blessed be Abram of the most high God, possessor of heaven and earth:

And blessed be the most high God, which hath delivered thine enemies into thy hand. And he gave him tithes of all.

Genesis 14:18-20

For this Melchisedec, king of Salem, priest of the most high God, who met Abraham returning from the slaughter of the kings, and blessed him;

To whom also Abraham gave a tenth part of all; first being by interpretation King of righteousness, and after that also King of Salem, which is, King of peace;

Without father, without mother, without descent, having neither beginning of days, nor end of life; but made like unto the Son of God; abideth a priest continually.

Now consider how great this man was, unto whom even the patriarch Abraham gave the tenth of the spoils.

And verily they that are of the sons of Levi, who receive the office of the priesthood, have a commandment to take tithes of the people according to the law, that is, of their brethren, though they come out of the loins of Abraham:

But he whose descent is not counted from them received

tithes of Abraham, and blessed him that had the promises.
And without all contradiction the less is blessed of the
better.

And here men that die receive tithes; but there he re-
ceiveth them, of whom it is witnessed that he liveth.

And as I may so say, Levi also, who receiveth tithes,
payed tithes in Abraham.   Hebrews 7:1-9

Several years later, but still way before the law of Moses
was given, Jacob vowed to God to pay tithes.

And Jacob vowed a vow, saying, If God will be with me,
and will keep me in this way that I go, and will give me
bread to eat, and raiment to put on,

So that I come again to my father's house in peace; then
shall the Lord be my God:

And this stone, which I have set for a pillar, shall be
God's house; and of all that thou shalt give me I will sure-
ly give the tenth unto thee.   Genesis 28:20-22

We find many references to paying tithes throughout the
Bible, 39 in all, not counting where it was referred to by
the word **tenth** instead of tithe. Tithing is referred to by
name seven times in the New Testament. It was also referred to without using the exact word tithe, tithes, or tithing several other times.

What was the purpose of the tithe; for what did the money collected go? The practice of tithing was used to support the Levites, the priests, the poor and needy, God's
house, and to honor God.

THE LEVITES:

But the tithes of the children of Israel, which they offer
as an heave offering unto the Lord, I have given to the
Levites to inherit: therefore I have said unto them, Among
the children of Israel they shall have no inheritance.
                                             Numbers 18:24

THE PRIESTS:

Thus speak unto the Levites, and say unto them, When ye
take of the children of Israel the tithes which I have given
you from them for your inheritance, then ye shall offer up

an heave offering of it for the Lord, even a tenth part of the tithe.

And this your heave offering shall be reckoned unto you, as though it were the corn of the threshing floor, and as the fulness of the winepress.

Thus ye also shall offer an heave offering unto the Lord of all your tithes, which ye receive of the children of Israel; and ye shall give thereof the Lord's heave offering to Aaron the priest.　　　　　Numbers 18:26-28

And that we should bring the first fruits of our dough, and our offerings, and the fruit of all manner of trees, of wine and of oil, unto the priests, to the chambers of the house of our God; and the tithes of our ground unto the Levites, that the same Levites might have the tithes in all the cities of our tillage.　　　　Nehemiah 10:37

THE POOR AND NEEDY:

And the Levite that is within thy gates; thou shalt not forsake him; for he hath no part nor inheritance with thee.

At the end of three years thou shalt bring forth all the tithes of thine increase the same year, and shalt lay it up within thy gates:

And the Levite, (because he hath no part nor inheritance with thee,) and the stranger, and the fatherless, and the widow, which are within thy gates, shall come, and shall eat and be satisfied; that the Lord thy God may bless thee in all the work of thine hand which thou doest.
　　　　　　　　　　　　　　　Deuteronomy 14:27-29

When thou hast made an end of tithing all the tithes of thine increase the third year, which is the year of tithing, and hast given it unto the Levite, the stranger, the fatherless, and the widow, that they may eat within thy gates, and be filled;

Then thou shalt say before the Lord thy God, I have brought away the hallowed things out of mine house, and also have given them unto the Levite, and unto the stranger, to the fatherless, and to the widow, according to all thy commandments which thou hast commanded me: I have not transgressed thy commandments, neither have I forgotten them: Deuteronomy 26:12,13

TO SUPPLY GOD'S HOUSE:

Bring ye all the tithes into the storehouse, that there may be meat in mine house, and prove me now herewith, saith the Lord of hosts, if I will not open you the windows of heaven, and pour you out a blessing, that there shall not be room enough to receive it. Malachi 3:10

TO HONOR GOD:

Honour the Lord with thy substance, and with the firstfruits of all thine increase: Proverbs 3:9

WHERE IS THE TITHE TO BE BROUGHT?

Then Hezekiah commanded to prepare chambers in the house of the Lord; and they prepared them,

And brought in the offerings and the tithes and the dedicated things faithfully; over which Cononiah the Levite was ruler, and Shimei his brother was the next.

II Chronicles 31:11,12

And the priest the son of Aaron shall be with the Levites, when the Levites take tithes; and the Levites shall bring up the tithe of the tithes unto the house of our God, to the chambers, into the treasure house. Nehemiah 10:38

Bring ye all the tithes into the storehouse, that there may be meat in mine house, and prove me now herewith, saith the Lord of hosts, if I will not open you the windows of heaven, and pour you out a blessing, that there shall not be room enough to receive it. Malachi 3:10

It is easy to see that the tithe is to be brought to God's house. In the Old Testament, the temple. In the New Testament, the church.

WHAT ABOUT TITHING IN THE NEW TESTAMENT?

CHRIST TAUGHT IT!

Woe unto you, scribes and Pharisees, hypocrites! for ye pay tithe of mint and anise and cummin, and have omitted the weightier matters of the law, judgment, mercy, and faith: these ought ye to have done, and not to leave the

59

other undone. Matthew 23:23

But woe unto you, Pharisees! for ye tithe mint and rue and all manner of herbs, and pass over judgment and the love of God: these ought ye to have done, and not to leave the other undone. Luke 11:42

The Pharisee stood and prayed thus with himself, God, I thank thee, that I am not as other men are, extortioners, unjust, adulterers, or even as this publican.

I fast twice in the week, I give tithes of all that I possess. Luke 18:11, 12

For I say unto you. That except your righteousness shall exceed the righteousness of the scribes and Pharisees, ye shall in no case enter into the kingdom of heaven. Matthew 5:20

Christ plainly teaches that tithe should be paid, but the other things should not be left undone. **Even hypocrites pay tithe.**

PAUL TAUGHT IT!

Thou that sayest a man should not commit adultery, dost thou commit adultery? thou that abhorrest idols, dost thou commit sacrilege? Romans 2:22

Committing sacrilege here is the same as robbing God in Malachi 3:10 or using the consecrated things for self.

Let him that is taught in the word communicate unto him that teacheth in all good things. Galatians 6:6

The word **communicate** in Galatians 6:6 is from the Greek word **koinoneo.** It refers to the material support of the ministry.

The next scripture reference is very clearly referring to tithing. In the light of the scripture we have already shared, it should be easily seen by the serious student of the Word. Watch closely.

Who goeth a warfare any time at his own charges? who planteth a vineyard, and eateth not of the fruit thereof? or who feedeth a flock, and eateth not of the milk of the flock?

Say I these things as a man? or saith not the law the

same also?

For it is written in the law of Moses, Thou shalt not muzzle the mouth of the ox that treadeth out the corn. Doth God take care for oxen?

Or saith he it altogether for our sakes? For our sakes, no doubt, this is written: that he that ploweth should plow in hope; and that he that thresheth in hope should be partaker of his hope.

If we have sown unto you spiritual things, is it a great thing if we shall reap your carnal things?

If others be partakers of this power over you, are not we rather? Nevertheless we have not used this power; but suffer all things, lest we should hinder the gospel of Christ.

Do ye not know that they which minister about holy things live of the things of the temple? and they which wait at the altar are partakers with the altar?

Even so hath the Lord ordained that they which preach the gospel should live of the gospel. I Corinthians 9:7-14

In verse 13 and 14, Paul compares the preacher of the gospel in the New Testament to the priest of the temple in the Old Testament.

Notice in verse 14 that Paul clearly confirms tithing in the New Testament when he says, **"Even so** hath the Lord ordained that they which preach the gospel should live of the gospel"

Many believers like to claim the blessings of Abraham.

Christ hath redeemed us from the curse of the law, being made a curse for us: for it is written, Cursed is every one that hangeth on a tree:

That the blessing of Abraham might come on the Gentiles through Jesus Christ; that we might receive the promise of the Spirit through faith. Galatians 3:13,14

If we as New Testament believers want to claim to be children of Abraham by faith, **we** need to walk in his steps.

And the father of circumcision to them who are not of the

61

circumcision only, but who also walk in the steps of that faith of our father Abraham, which he had being yet uncircumcised. Romans 4:12

Tithing is proof of obedience and appreciation of God's blessings.

Charge them that are rich in this world, that they be not highminded, nor trust in uncertain riches, but in the living God, who giveth us richly all things to enjoy;

That they do good, that they be rich in good works, ready to distribute, willing to communicate;

I Timothy 6:17, 18

There are spiritual and material blessings promised to the tither.

Honour the Lord with thy substance, and with the firstfruits of all thine increase:

So shall thy barns be filled with plenty, and thy presses shall burst out with new wine. Proverbs 3:9,10

Bring ye all the tithes into the storehouse, that there may be meat in mine house, and prove me now herewith, saith the Lord of hosts, if I will not open you the windows of heaven, and pour you out a blessing, that there shall not be room enough to receive it. Malachi 3:10

And it shall come to pass, if thou shalt hearken diligently unto the voice of the Lord thy God, to observe and to do all his commandments which I command thee this day, that the Lord thy God will set thee on high above all nations of the earth:

And all these blessings shall come on thee, and overtake thee, if thou shalt hearken unto the voice of the Lord thy God.

Blessed shalt thou be in the city, and blessed shalt thou be in the field.

Blessed shall be the fruit of thy body, and the fruit of thy ground, and the fruit of thy cattle, the increase of thy kine, and the flocks of thy sheep.

Blessed shall be thy basket and thy store.

Blessed shalt thou be when thou comest in, and blessed

shalt thou be when thou goest out.

The Lord shall cause thine enemies that rise up against thee to be smitten before thy face: they shall come out against thee one way, and flee before thee seven ways.

The Lord shall command the blessing upon thee in thy storehouses, and in all that thou settest thine hand unto; and he shall bless thee in the land which the Lord thy God giveth thee.

And the Lord shall make thee the head, and not the tail; and thou shalt be above only, and thou shalt not be beneath; if that thou hearken unto the commandments of the Lord thy God, which I command thee this day, to observe and to do them: Deuteronomy 28:1-8,13

Why is there so much confusion and resistance to tithing among today's believers? I believe the answer is obvious. SELFISHNESS!

Many people are too stingy to pay God what they owe Him, but in the end, they do not get to spend the money themselves. The doctor or hospital gets it, or the divorce lawyer, or the mental institution. Consider the following:

But it shall come to pass, if thou wilt not hearken unto the voice of the Lord thy God, to observe to do all his commandments and his statutes which I command thee this day; that all these curses shall come upon thee, and overtake thee:

Cursed shalt thou be in the city, and cursed shalt thou be in the field.

Cursed shall be thy basket and thy store.

Cursed shall be the fruit of thy body, and the fruit of thy land, the increase of thy kine, and the flocks of thy sheep.

Cursed shalt thou be when thou comest in, and cursed shalt thou be when thou goest out.

The Lord shall send upon thee cursing, vexation, and rebuke, in all that thou settest thine hand unto for to do, until thou be destroyed, and until thou perish quickly; because of the wickedness of thy doings, whereby thou hast forsaken me.

The Lord shall make the pestilence cleave unto thee, un-

til he have consumed thee from off the land, whither thou goest to possess it.

Thou shalt betroth a wife, and another man shall lie with her; thou shalt build an house, and thou shalt not dwell therein: Thou shalt plant a vineyard, and shalt not gather the grapes thereof.

Thy sons and thy daughters shall be given unto another people, and thine eyes shall look, and fail with longing for them all the day long: and there shall be no might in thine hand.

Moreover all these curses shall come upon thee, and shall pursue thee, and overtake thee, till thou be destroyed; because thou hearkenedst not unto the voice of the Lord thy God, to keep his commandments and his statutes which he commanded thee:

Deuteronomy 28:15-21, 30, 32, 45

I personally consider tithing one of the greatest ways to worship God. I remember seeing a bumper sticker with the slogan, "IF YOU LOVE JESUS, HONK!" I say if you love Jesus, tithe. It costs nothing to honk. Any old lukewarm Christian can lift their hands and mouth a few "hallelujahs" or "praise the Lords," but it costs something to tithe. When a person tithes, that person is giving up the product of his or her strength, talent, or wisdom. They are saying, "Here, God, is one-tenth of a big part of my life."

The person who refuses to pay God the tithe, yet claims to be righteous and holy, is deceiving himself. He has the father of all sins in his heart — the love of money.

For the love of money is the root of all evil: which while some coveted after, they have erred from the faith, and pierced themselves through with many sorrows.

I Timothy 6:10

As we said before, so say I now again. If any man preach any other gospel unto you than that ye have received, let him be accursed.

Galatians 1:9

7
HOLINESS

In the Epistles of Paul, we find the word **holy** 42 times, **holiness** 9 times, **righteous** 8 times, and **righteousness** 63 times. If you count Hebrews as having been written by Paul, you can raise those numbers.

The word **holy** is found in the entire Bible 596 times; **holiness** 45 times; **righteous** 236 times; **righteousness** 300 times; and **sanctify, sanctified,** and **sanctification** a total of 136 times.

It might be interesting to note that the word **sanctification** is found only in the New Testament, and that only five times, and four of those times are by Paul.

Holy, holiness, righteous, righteousness, sanctify, and sanctification all mean basically the same thing:

"Perfection, spiritually pure, set apart to a sacred purpose or to religious use, consecrated, dedicated, innocent, just, lawful, cleansed."

Some will differ with me as to the difference between righteousness and holiness. I will not quarrel with that for I respect their opinion. But, basically it still comes back to being right with God, and we cannot be right with God without being **holy.**

We must realize, however, that there is a difference between **justification** and **holiness.** Some are making a shipwreck of their faith by believing the lie that **justification** places them in the position of **holiness** to the extent **they** need never do any more to perfect **holiness** after they are **justified,** or **saved.** (See Chapter Four, "The Big Lie," in my book, **What Is Holiness?**)

God commanded those in the Old Testament to be **holy.**

For I am the Lord your God: ye shall therefore sanctify yourselves, and ye shall be holy; for I am holy: neither shall ye defile yourselves with any manner of creeping thing that creepeth upon the earth. Leviticus 11:44

The Apostle Peter reminds us of this in the New Testament.

But as he which hath called you is holy, so be ye holy in all manner of conversation;
Because it is written, Be ye holy; for I am holy.

I Peter 1:15, 16

If you will notice the context of both of these passages, you will find there is something the reader must do to be **holy.**

Therein lies the grave mistake many teachers and preachers are spreading today, and that is that **holiness** is given to us automatically and there is nothing we can do to make ourselves **holy.**

Obviously, they are not seeing clearly enough to understand the difference between **holiness** and justification.

Paul talks of justification in the book of Romans and many people have completely misunderstood his message.

What shall we say then that Abraham our father, as pertaining to the flesh, hath found?
For if Abraham were justified by works, he hath whereof to glory; but not before God.
For what saith the scripture? Abraham believed God, and it was counted unto him for righteousness.
Now to him that worketh is the reward not reckoned of grace, but of debt.
But to him that worketh not, but believeth on him that justifieth the ungodly, his faith is counted for righteousness.

Romans 4:1-5

The words **justified** and **justification** mean "to be acquitted, to be innocent, free from sin."

When Abraham was **justified** by faith it brought him to a place of "acquittal," "freedom" from his past sins, or as so many like to define **justified,** JUST-AS-IF-IED never sinned.

But you see, **justification** only brings you to the starting line of your Christian experience. As great as **justifica-**

66

tion or salvation is, it is **not the end of the race,** it is **only the start.**

Because many have misunderstood the fourth chapter of Romans, a great number of people have ceased to believe that living a life within holiness standards is necessary.

A great number of ministers have ceased preaching against sin and worldliness. Because they mistakenly believe a person is as holy as he will ever be when he receives Christ as his Savior, they frustrate the working of God's holiness in many people.

Again, let me say that justification, as wonderful as it is, only brings us to the starting line of the Christian race.

The argument that you can never be any more perfect than when you arise from the place of prayer where you are made clean by the blood of Jesus Christ is a good argument. Truthfully, we are redeemed, justified, or born again because of faith in Christ's work on the cross, and not by our own good works.

For by grace are ye saved through faith; and that not of yourselves: it is the gift of God:

Not of works, lest any man should boast.

Ephesians 2:8, 9

But let's not stop there.

*For we are his workmanship, created in Christ Jesus **unto good works**, which God hath before ordained that we should **walk in them**.*   Ephesians 2:10

It is true, you can never make yourself good enough to be accepted into the family of God, you must be born into that family by the Spirit of God.

But it is just like the little baby who is born, and the doctor comes out to tell us the baby is perfect. All it can do is cry, throw up, and make messes. Yet, that baby is declared perfect. However, if in a certain period of time that baby does not begin to pull itself up, or walk, or talk, we know that the baby has not retained its state of perfection, because it has ceased to grow and make normal progress.

We take that baby to the doctor and want to know what is wrong. **How do we know** something is wrong? We can easily determine that the baby is no longer perfect **because it is not making normal progress**. Perfection in this instance means growth, improvement, and coming to maturity.

Be ye therefore perfect, even as your Father which is in heaven is perfect. Matthew 5:48

These words of Jesus are talking about labor, growth, and completeness as we mature and make forward progress. So you see, if we do not continue to grow, to labor and mature, we who were once perfect become imperfect.

Many have been misled into believing that if they try to make themselves better by living a holy life, they are in danger of falling from (or at least frustrating) grace.

How can such teachers ignore scriptures such as the following?

Wherefore, my beloved, as ye have always obeyed, not as in my presence only, but now much more in my absence, **work out** *your own salvation with fear and trembling.*

Philippians 2:12

The preceding verse, by the way, is written by the Apostle Paul, the same man who, under the inspiration of the Holy Spirit, wrote Romans 4:1-8.

There is no contradiction here, not at all. You see, in one place, Romans 4:1-8, he is talking of being saved; in the other, Philippians 2:12, he is talking about necessary growth after salvation, or justification.

Again, there is no contradiction or discrepancy in the two teachings: **one**, that there is absolutely nothing you can do to make yourself good enough to be saved; **two**, that you yourself must do something if you are to stay in the grace of God.

The **problem** arises either when the **sinner** tries to earn **his** salvation, or when the **Christian** ignores **his** responsibility to keep himself in the grace of God and perfect holiness in his life.

What is so amazing is that so-called Bible teachers and expositors not only cannot see this truth, they fight against it.

Many loudly proclaim there is nothing we can do to keep ourselves. We are kept by His grace and His love. The truth is that we must **keep ourselves** in **His grace,** and in **His love.**

Consider the following wide range of Bible authors.

JESUS:

Then said Jesus to those Jews which believed on him, If ye continue in my word, then are ye my disciples indeed.

John 8:31

He that hath my commandments, and keepeth them, he it is that loveth me: and he that loveth me shall be loved by my Father, and I will love him, and will manifest myself to him,

Jesus answered and said unto him, If a man love me, he will keep my words: and my Father will love him, and we will come unto him, and make our abode with him

John 14:21, 23

If ye keep my commandments, ye shall abide in my love; even as I have kept my Father's commandment, and abide in his love.   John 15:10

He that overcometh, the same shall be clothed in white raiment; and I will not blot out his name out of the book of life, but I will confess his name before my Father, and before his angels.   Revelation 3:5

PAUL:

But I keep under my body, and bring it into subjection: lest that by any means, when I have preached to others, I myself should be a castaway.   I Corinthians 9:27

Lay hands suddenly on no man, neither be partaker of other men's sins: keep thyself pure.   I Timothy 5:22

JOHN:

And hereby we do know that we know him, if we keep his commandments.

He that saith, I know him, and keepeth not his commandments, is a liar, and the truth is not in him.

But whoso keepeth his word, in him verily is the love of

God perfected: hereby know we that we are in him.

I John 2:3-5

In this the children of God are manifest, and the children of the devil: whosoever doeth not righteousness is not of God, neither he that loveth not his brother.

I John 3:10

JUDE:

But ye, beloved, building up yourselves on your most holy faith, praying in the Holy Ghost,

Keep yourselves in the love of God, looking for the mercy of our Lord Jesus Christ unto eternal life.   Jude 20, 21

THE ANGEL:

Here is the patience of the saints: here are they that keep the commandments of God, and the faith of Jesus.

Revelation 14:12

Blessed are they that do his commandments, that they may have right to the tree of life, and may enter in through the gates into the city.   Revelation 22:14

And these are but a sampling of scriptures.

How can any **serious** student of God's word, any sincere follower of Jesus Christ, miss this truth which is taught throughout the entire Bible: that a follower of God must work, labor, and strive to keep himself in the grace and love of God?

Not every one that saith unto me, Lord, Lord, shall enter into the kingdom of heaven; but he that doeth the will of my Father which is in heaven.

Many will say to me in that day, Lord, Lord, have we not prophesied in thy name? and in thy name cast out devils? and in thy name done many wonderful works?

And then will I profess unto them, I never knew you: depart from me, ye that work iniquity.   Matthew 7:21-23

Strive to enter in at the strait gate: for many, I say unto you, will seek to enter in, and shall not be able.

Luke 13:24

Whereby are given unto us exceeding great and precious promises: that by these ye might be partakers of the di-

70

vine nature, having escaped the corruption that is in the world through lust.

And beside this, giving all diligence, add to your faith virtue; and to virtue knowledge;

And to knowledge temperance; and to temperance patience; and to patience godliness;

And to godliness brotherly kindness; and to brotherly kindness charity.

For if these things be in you, and abound, they make you that ye shall neither be barren nor unfruitful in the knowledge of our Lord Jesus Christ.

But he that lacketh these things is blind, and cannot see afar off, and hath forgotten that he was purged from his old sins.

Wherefore the rather, brethren, give diligence to make your calling and election sure: for if ye do these things, ye shall never fall.   II Peter 1:4-10

Oh yes, I know, I understand:

Who are kept by the power of God through faith unto salvation ready to be revealed in the last time.

I Peter 1:5

We **must understand** that it is our responsibility to keep ourselves where God's grace, love, and power can continue to work in our lives.

The wonderful truth here lies in the fact that, as we labor to keep ourselves in the grace of God, that grace becomes more and more precious to us. Even as we make our sometimes feeble efforts, the truth comes bounding back to us: that were it not for God's great grace, we wouldn't even care to make those efforts. And as we are made to think more of His grace, oh, how we are stirred to rejoicing.

As we said before, so say I now again, If any man preach any other gospel unto you than that ye have received, let him be accursed.   Galatians 1:9

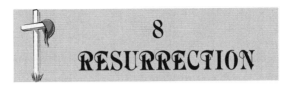

8
RESURRECTION

If a man die, shall he live again...?   Job 14:14

The question of a resurrection has troubled mankind for thousands of years.

In fact, the resurrection, for many, is still but a mystery. The Apostle Paul seems to be mightily used of God to reveal to us spiritual mysteries.

Behold, I shew you a mystery; We shall not all sleep, but we shall all be changed.   I Corinthians 15:51

The words **mystery** and **mysteries** are found in the Bible only in the New Testament. The two words are mentioned only 27 times and 21 of those times are in Paul's writings.

A dictionary definition of the word **mystery** reads: "a religious truth that man can know by revelation alone and cannot fully understand."[1]

Paul, the great revealer of secrets, tells us much of the resurrection.

But first, let's hear from others concerning this important subject.

For I know that my redeemer liveth, and that he shall stand at the later day upon the earth:

And though after my skin worms destroy this body, yet in my flesh shall I see God;

Whom I shall see for myself, and mine eyes shall behold, and not another; Though my reins be consumed within me.   Job 19:25-27

For thou wilt not leave my soul in hell; neither wilt thou suffer thine Holy One to see corruption.   Psalms 16:10

Thy dead men shall live, together with my dead body shall they arise. Awake and sing, ye that dwell in dust: for thy dew is as the dew of herbs, and the earth shall cast out the dead.   Isaiah 26:19

And many of them that sleep in the dust of the earth shall awake, some to everlasting life, and some to shame and everlasting contempt.   Daniel 12:2

From that time forth began Jesus to shew unto his disciples, how that he must go unto Jerusalem, and suffer many things of the elders and chief priests and scribes, and be killed, and be raised again the third day.

Matthew 16:21

Martha saith unto him, I know that he shall rise again in the resurrection at the last day.   John 11:24

Men and brethren, let me freely speak unto you of the patriarch David, that he is both dead and buried, and his sepulchre is with us unto this day.

Therefore being a prophet, and knowing that God had sworn with an oath to him, that of the fruit of his loins, according to the flesh, he would raise up Christ to sit on his throne;

He seeing this before spake of the resurrection of Christ, that his soul was not left in hell, neither his flesh did see corruption.   Acts 2:29-31

Women received their dead raised to life again: and others were tortured, not accepting deliverance; that they might obtain a better resurrection: Hebrews 11:35

Blessed be the God and Father of our Lord Jesus Christ, which according to his abundant mercy hath begotten us again unto a lively hope by the resurrection of Jesus Christ from the dead,   I Peter 1:3

There is a large volume of material on the resurrection, but it seems Paul has been chosen by God to reveal intricate details.

Let us examine carefully I Corinthians, Chapter 15.

In verses 1 through 8, Paul tells us of the death, burial, and resurrection of Jesus Christ. Verses 12 through 19 reveal to us the **importance** of the resurrection.

But if there be no resurrection of the dead, then is Christ not risen:

And if Christ be not risen, then is our preaching vain, and your faith is also vain.

And if Christ be not raised, your faith is vain; ye are yet in your sins. I Corinthians 15:13, 14, 17

The **certainty** of the resurrection is dealt with from verses 20 through 22.

But now is Christ risen from the dead, and become the firstfruits of them that slept.

For since by man came death, by man came also the resurrection of the dead.

For as in Adam all die, even so in Christ shall all be made alive. I Corinthians 15:20-22

Paul tells the **order** and **time** of the resurrection in verse 23.

But every man in his own order: Christ the firstfruits; afterward they that are Christ's at his coming.

I Corinthians 15:23

In verses 35 through 38, we read of the **method** of resurrection.

But some man will say, How are the dead raised up? and with what body do they come?

Thou fool, that which thou sowest is not quickened, except it die:

And that which thou sowest, thou sowest not that body that shall be, but bare grain, it may chance of wheat, or of some other grain:

But God giveth it a body as it hath pleased him, and to every seed his own body. I Corinthians 15:35-38

And what will be the **nature** of the resurrected bodies?

All flesh is not the same flesh: but there is one kind of flesh of men, another flesh of beasts, another of fishes, and another of birds.

So also is the resurrection of the dead. It is sown in corruption; it is raised in incorruption:

It is sown in dishonour; it is raised in glory: it is sown in weakness; it is raised in power:

It is sown a natural body; it is raised a spiritual body. There is a natural body, and there is a spiritual body.

I Corinthians 15:39, 42-44

The **necessity** of a resurrection is also given to us in this chapter.

And so it is written, The first man Adam was made a living soul; the last Adam was made a quickening spirit.

Howbeit that was not first which is spiritual, but that which is natural; and afterward that which is spiritual.

The first man is of the earth, earthy: the second man is the Lord from heaven.

As is the earthy, such are they also that are earthy: and as is the heavenly, such are they also that are heavenly.

And as we have borne the image of the earthy, we shall also bear the image of the heavenly.

Now this I say, brethren, that flesh and blood cannot inherit the kingdom of God; neither doth corruption inherit incorruption. I Corinthians 15:45-50

And then Paul reveals to us the mystery, that which before had been kept a secret.

Behold, I shew you a mystery; We shall not all sleep, but we shall all be changed. I Corinthians 15:51

What is Paul telling us here? What new truth is this? This is one of the revelations God has chosen Paul to deliver, the times and manner of the resurrection. Not everyone will die physically. Some will be given resurrection bodies, or in other words, changed from mortality to immortality, from corruptible bodies to incorruptible bodies in an instant, and that without going the way of death and the grave.

But I would not have you to be ignorant, brethren, concerning them which are asleep, that ye sorrow not, even as others which have no hope.

For if we believe that Jesus died and rose again, even so them also which sleep in Jesus will God bring with him.

For this we say unto you by the word of the Lord, that we which are alive and remain unto the coming of the Lord shall not prevent them which are asleep.

For the Lord himself shall descend from heaven with a shout with the voice of the archangel, and with the trump of God: and the dead in Christ shall rise first:

Then we which are alive and remain shall be caught up

together with them in the clouds, to meet the Lord in the air: and so shall we ever be with the Lord.

Wherefore comfort one another with these words.

I Thessalonians 4:13-18

Behold, I shew you a mystery; We shall not all sleep, but we shall all be changed.

In a moment, in the twinkling of an eye, at the last trump: for the trumpet shall sound, and the dead shall be raised incorruptible, and we shall be changed.

For this corruptible must put on incorruption, and this mortal must put on immortality.

So when this corruptible shall have put on incorruption, and this mortal shall have put on immortality, then shall be brought to pass the saying that is written, Death is swallowed up in victory. I Corinthians 15:51-54

Paul sums up the fifteenth chapter of I Corinthians by giving us a "Therefore," or, in other words, "Because of this."

Therefore, my beloved brethren, be ye stedfast, unmoveable, always abounding in the work of the Lord, forasmuch as ye know that your labour is not in vain in the Lord. I Corinthians 15:58

Is it true then, that while our bodies are lying in the grave, waiting for the resurrection, our souls are asleep, or unconscious? Paul gives us insight into this matter also.

For we know that if our earthly house of this tabernacle were dissolved, we have a building of God, an house not made with hands, eternal in the heavens.

For in this we groan, earnestly desiring to be clothed upon with our house which is from heaven:

If so be that being clothed we shall not be found naked.

For we that are in this tabernacle do groan, being burdened: not for that we would be unclothed, but clothed upon, that mortality might be swallowed up of life.

Now he that hath wrought us for the selfsame thing is God, who also hath given unto us the earnest of the Spirit.

Therefore we are always confident, knowing that, whilst

we are at home in the body, we are absent from the Lord:
(For we walk by faith, not by sight:)
*We are confident, I say, and willing rather to be absent
from the body, and to be present with the Lord.*

II Corinthians 5:1-8
Such clear teaching wipes away all the doubt on subjects
such as "soulsleep." It matters not what man or organiza-
tion preaches, God's Word and God's Word alone must be
our guide.

To die and be absent from the body means we go to
heaven to be with the Lord.

For to me to live is Christ, and to die is gain.

Philippians 1:21
*For as the body without the spirit is dead, so faith with-
out works is dead also.*   James 2:26
*And when he had opened the fifth seal, I saw under the
altar the souls of them that were slain for the word of
God, and for the testimony which they held.*
*And they cried with a loud voice, saying, HOW long, 0
Lord, holy and true, dost thou not judge and avenge our
blood on them that dwell on the earth?*
*And white robes were given unto every one of them; and
it was said unto them, that they should rest yet for a little
season, until their fellow servants also and their brethren,
that should be killed as they were, should be fulfilled.*

Revelation 6:9-11
These and other scriptures are given to clearly show us
that the inner man does not go to the grave at death, but to
heaven if one is righteous. If a person is wicked, he goes
to hell to await the resurrection of his body.

There are organizations which teach that when man dies,
he dies like a dog, or other animal. In other words, his
body goes to the ground. He knows nothing more. Those
who teach this doctrine erroneously quote from the book
of Ecclesiastes in an attempt to prove their point.

*I said in mine heart concerning the estate of the sons of
men, that God might manifest them, and that they might
see that they themselves are beasts.*

77

For that which befalleth the sons of men befalleth beasts; even one thing befalleth them: as the one dieth, so dieth the other; yea, they have all one breath; so that a man hath no preeminence above a beast: for all is vanity.

All go unto one place; all are of the dusts, and all turn to dust again.   Ecclesiastes 3:18-20

But even here, if they would continue on just one more verse, they would disprove their own false teaching.

Who knoweth the spirit of man that goeth upward, and the spirit of the beast that goeth downward to the earth?

Ecclesiastes 3:21

Also, there is a **first** resurrection, and a **second** resurrection.

The **first** resurrection is for the believers who lived a holy life here on earth.

And I saw thrones, and they sat upon them, and judgment was given unto them: and I saw the souls of them that were beheaded for the witness of Jesus, and for the word of God, and which had not worshipped the beast, neither his image, neither had received his mark upon their foreheads, or in their hands; and they lived and reigned with Christ a thousand years.

But the rest of the dead lived not again until the thousand years were finished. This is the first resurrection.

Blessed and holy is he that hath part in the first resurrection: on such the second death hath no power, but they shall be priests of God and of Christ, and shall reign with him a thousand years.   Revelation 20:4-6

The **second** resurrection is to bring the dead up from hell to stand before the great white throne for this final judgment, and then the wicked dead will be cast into the lake of fire that God calls the second death.

And I saw a great white throne, and him that sat on it, from whose face the earth and the heaven fled away; and there was found no place for them.

And I saw the dead, small and great, stand before God; and the books were opened: and another book was opened, which is the book of life: and the dead were judged out of those things which were written in the books, according to their works.

And the sea gave up the dead which were in it; and death and hell delivered up the dead which were in them: and they were judged every man according to their works.

And death and hell were cast into the lake of fire. This is the second death.

And whosoever was not found written in the book of life was cast into the lake of fire. Revelation 20:11-15

Let me remind you here that the second death is not talking about annihilation. Some, because of their aversion and great fear of hell, have invented a doctrine called annihilation, which teaches that the wicked will simply be destroyed and never know anything after that destruction.

In their desire to flee, not from hell, but from the teachings of hell, they have invented a doctrine to soothe their conscience. However, that doctrine is totally false. We need only to consult divine scripture to debunk that foolish doctrine.

And the third angel followed them saying with a loud voice, If any man worship the beast and his image, and receive his mark in his forehead, or in his hand,

The same shall drink of the wine of the wrath- of God, which is poured out without mixture into the cup of his indignation; and he shall be tormented with fire and brimstone in the presence of the holy angels, and in the presence of the Lamb:

And the smoke of their torment ascendeth up for ever and ever: and they have no rest day nor night, who worship the beast and his image, and whosoever receiveth the mark of his name. Revelation 14:9-11

And if thy hand offend thee, cut it off: it is better for thee to enter into life maimed, than having two hands to go into hell, into the fire that never shall be quenched:

Where their worm dieth not, and the fire is not quenched.

And if thy foot offend thee, cut it off: it is better for thee to enter halt into life, than having two feet to be cast into hell, into the fire that never shall be quenched:

Where their worm dieth not, and the fire is not quenched.

And if thine eye offend thee, pluck it out: it is better for thee to enter into the kingdom of God with one eye, than having two eyes to be cast into hell fire:

Where their worm dieth not, and the fire is not quenched. Mark 9:43-48

Sometimes, in our desire to smooth things over for the timid and squeamish, we invent our own little doctrines. How many times has it been told that once we get into the presence of the Lord, we will never even remember those in hell, or the lake of fire? This is just another unscriptural teaching man has invented. Let's see what God has to say.

The same shall drink of the wine of the wrath of God, which is poured out without mixture into the cup of his indignation; and he shall be tormented with fire and brimstone in the presence of the holy angels, and in the presence of the Lamb: Revelation 14:10

For as the new heavens and the new earth, which I will make, shall remain before me, saith the Lord, so shall your seed and your name remain.

And it shall come to pass, that from one new moon to another, and from one sabbath to another, shall all flesh come to worship before me, saith the Lord.

*And they shall go forth, and look upon the carcases of the men that have transgressed against me: for their worm shall not **die** neither shall their fire be quenched; and they shall be an abhorring unto all flesh.*

Isaiah 66:22-24

Some will protest, saying, how can we be happy if we know some of our loved ones are in torment? Here is where the great wisdom and power of God proves itself to be sufficient.

The purpose of this opening to hell, or the lake of fire, will be to cause coming generations to abhor sin and its consequences. When men can see into hell, it will be a great warning to them to continue to walk in the ways of God. As horrifying as this thought may seem to us now, let us not doubt the wisdom of God as He prepares His plan to keep eternal generations in line with His laws and commandments.

Again I say, it matters not what men and their organizations teach, God's Word and God's Word alone must be our guide.

As we said before, so say I now again, If any man preach any other gospel unto you than that ye have received, let him be accursed. Galatians 1:9

1. Merriam-Webster Classics Edition Dictionary, 1972, G. & C. Merriam Company.

9
FUTURE EVENTS

In this chapter concerning future events, I would like to first deal with the controversial subject of the rapture.

But I would not have you to be ignorant, brethren, concerning them which are asleep, that ye sorrow not, even as others which have no hope.

For if we believe that Jesus died and rose again, even so them also which sleep in Jesus will God bring with him.

For this we say unto you by the word of the Lord, that we which are alive and remain unto the coming of the Lord shall not prevent them which are asleep.

For the Lord himself shall descend from heaven with a shout, with the voice of the archangel, and with the trump of God: and the dead in Christ shall rise first:

Then we which are alive and remain shall be caught up together with them in the clouds, to meet the Lord in the air: and so shall we ever be with the Lord.

Wherefore comfort one another with these words.

I Thessalonians 4:13-18

One of the reasons the subject of the rapture is controversial is that the word **rapture,** like the word **trinity,** cannot be found in the Bible. But then, as we have pointed out before, the word **Bible** cannot be found in the Bible.

We actually get the word **rapture** from the Greek word **harpazo,** which means "to carry off, grasp hastily; snatch up; to seize and overpower." From this we get our word **rapture.**

The rapture differs from the second coming of Christ in that at the second coming Christ comes all the way back to the earth to set up residence. At the rapture. He comes part of the way back; and the raptured, or caught-up ones, meet him in the air.

For the Lord himself shall descend from heaven with a

shout, with the voice of the archangel, and with the trump of God: and the dead in Christ shall rise first:

Then we which are alive and remain shall be caught up together with them in the clouds, to meet the Lord in the air: and so shall we ever be with the Lord.

I Thessalonians 4:16, 17

There is much controversy on the timing of this rapture Paul talks about. The church world is divided on whether the rapture will occur just before the seven-year tribulation period, at the end of the seven-year tribulation, or in the middle.

I have always believed the scripture gives evidence the rapture will be at the beginning of the tribulation, or just before.

For the past few years, however, I have been qualifying that teaching with the admonition that if the church would be called upon to go through the first three and a half years, or even through the entire seven years, the same grace that is keeping us now would be sufficient then.

And he said unto me, My grace is sufficient for thee: for my strength is made perfect in weakness ...

II Corinthians 12:9

Let us look at some of the scripture passages which at the very least suggest a rapture.

*Let not your heart be troubled: ye believe in **God,** believe also in me.*

In my Father's house are many mansions:
if it were not so, I would have told you. I go to prepare a place for you.

And if I go and prepare a place for you, I will come again, and receive you unto myself; that where I am, there ye may be also.			John 14:1-3

Behold, I shew you a mystery; We shall not all sleep, but we shall all be changed,

In a moment, in the twinkling of an eye, at the last trump: for the trumpet shall sound, and the dead shall be raised incorruptible, and we shall be changed.

I Corinthians 15:51-52

For what is our hope, or joy, or crown of rejoicing? Are not even ye in the presence of our Lord Jesus Christ at his coming? I Thessalonians 2:19

To the end he may stablish your hearts unblameable in holiness before God, even our Father, at the coming of our Lord Jesus Christ with all his saints.

I Thessalonians 3:13

For God hath not appointed us to wrath, but to obtain salvation by our Lord Jesus Christ,

I Thessalonians 5:9

And the very God of peace sanctify you wholly; and I pray God your whole spirit and soul and body be preserved blameless unto the coming of our Lord Jesus Christ. I Thessalonians 5:23

Now, let us look at some scriptures which suggest that the rapture is to take Christians out of the world before the tribulation period.

Watch ye therefore, and pray always, that ye may be accounted worthy to escape all these things that shall come to pass, and to stand before the Son of man. Luke 21:36

After this I looked, and, behold, a door was opened in heaven: and the first voice which I heard was as it were of a trumpet talking with me; which said, Come up hither, and I will shew thee things which must be hereafter.

Revelation 4:1

Seventy weeks are determined upon thy people and upon thy holy city, to finish the transgression, and to make an end of sins, and to make reconciliation for iniquity, and to bring in everlasting righteousness, and to seal up the vision and prophecy, and to anoint the most Holy.

Know therefore and understand, that from the going forth of the commandment to restore and to build Jerusalem unto the Messiah the Prince shall be seven weeks, and threescore and two weeks: the street shall be built again, and the wall, even in troublous times.

And after threescore and two weeks shall Messiah be cut off, but not for himself: and the people of the prince that shall come shall destroy the city and the sanctuary; and the end thereof shall be with a flood, and unto the end of the war desolations are determined.

And he shall confirm the covenant with many for one week: and in the midst of the week he shall cause the sacrifice and the oblation to cease, and for the overspreading of abominations he shall make it desolate, even until the consummation, and that determined shall be poured upon the desolate.   Daniel 9:24-27

The seventy weeks in the preceding scriptures literally mean seventy sevens; in fact, seventy sevens of years, or four hundred ninety years.

In the first year of his reign I Daniel understood by books the number of the years, whereof the word of the Lord came to Jeremiah the prophet, that he would accomplish seventy years in the desolations of Jerusalem.

Daniel 9:2

Notice that Daniel understood "by books the number of the years," and not the number of the days.

Notice also in Daniel 9:24 the words, "Seventy weeks are determined upon **thy** people and upon **thy** holy city."

Remember, the words are given to Daniel, and to the city of Jerusalem, and not to the Gentiles.

As we read Daniel 9:25, we see again that the prophecy is dealing with Jerusalem, and with Daniel's people.

Now, let me give the scriptures again; this time taking the liberty to underline **and** insert parenthetical words for the purpose of explanation.

Know therefore and understand, that from the going forth of the commandment to restore and to build Jerusalem unto the Messiah the Prince (the one the Jews were looking for) *shall be seven weeks* (seven weeks of years, or seven times seven equal forty-nine years), *and threescore and two weeks* (or, sixty-two times seven years equal four hundred thirty four years): *the street shall be built again, and the wall, even in troublous times.*

And after threescore and two weeks (seven times seven

equal forty-nine, sixty-two times seven equal four hundred and thirty-four, total, four hundred eighty-three years) *shall Messiah be cut off* (crucified), *but not for himself: and the people of the prince that shall come shall destroy the city and the sanctuary* (at this time, the counting of the seventy weeks of years has been put on hold at four hundred eighty-three years, and will stay on hold until the antichrist comes); *and the end thereof shall be with a flood, and unto the end of the war desolations are determined.*

And he (the antichrist) *shall confirm the covenant with many for one week* (seven years): *and in the midst of the week* (after three and one-half years) *he shall cause the sacrifice and the oblation to cease, and for the overspreading of abominations he shall make it desolate* (Matthew 24:15-21), *even until the consummation, and that determined shall be poured upon the desolate.*

Daniel 9:25-27

The serious students of Bible prophecy know that the books of Daniel and Revelation are tied together and need each other for interpretation. Therefore, let's look at some verses in Revelation, as well as Daniel, to bear out the truth of the seven year (actual years) tribulation period.

And I heard the man clothed in linen, which was upon the waters of the river, when he held up his right hand and his left hand unto heaven, and sware by him that liveth for ever that it shall be for a time, times, and an half; and when he shall have accomplished to scatter the power of the holy people, all these things shall be finished. Daniel 12:7

And there was given me a reed like unto a rod: and the angel stood, saying, Rise, and measure the temple of God, and the altar, and them that worship therein.

But the court which is without the temple leave out, and measure it not; for it is given unto the Gentiles: and the holy city shall they tread under foot forty and two months.

And I will give power unto my two witnesses, and they

shall prophesy a thousand two hundred and threescore days, clothed in sackcloth.   Revelation 11:1-3

And the woman fled into the wilderness, where she hath a place prepared of God, that they should feed her there a thousand two hundred and threescore days.
                                                    Revelation 12:6

And to the woman were given two wings of a great eagle, that she might fly into the wilderness, into her place, where she is nourished for a time, and times, and half a time, from the face of the serpent.   Revelation 12:14

And there was given unto him a mouth speaking great things and blasphemies; and power was given unto him to continue forty and two months.   Revelation 13:5

THE DIVINE ORDER OF EVENTS SEEMS TO BE:

(1) The rapture of the saints, getting them out of the world while God deals with the Jews.

Watch ye therefore, and pray always, that ye may be accounted worthy to escape all these things that shall come to pass, and to stand before the Son of man.
                                                    Luke 21:36

Which also said, Ye men of Galilee, why stand ye gazing up into heaven? this same Jesus, which is taken up from you into heaven, shall so come in like manner as ye have seen him go into heaven.   Acts 1:11

Wherefore he saith. Awake thou that sleepest, and arise from the dead, and Christ shall give thee light.

See then that ye walk circumspectly, not as fools, but as wise,

Redeeming the time, because the days are evil.
                                                    Ephesians 5:14-16

For the Lord himself shall descend from heaven with a shout, with the voice of the archangel, and with the trump of God: and the dead in Christ shall rise first:

Then we which are alive and remain shall be caught up together with them in the clouds, to meet the Lord in the air: and so shall we ever be with the Lord.
                                                    I Thessalonians 4:16,17

(2) The seven year tribulation period, when God deals essentially and especially with the Jews.

As I live, saith the Lord God, surely with a mighty hand, and with a stretched out arm, and with fury poured out, will I rule over you:

And I will bring you out from the people, and will gather you out of the countries wherein ye are scattered, with a mighty hand, and with a stretched out arm, and with fury poured out.

And I will bring you into the wilderness of the people, and there will I plead with you face to face.

Like as I pleaded with your fathers in the wilderness of the land of Egypt, so will I plead with you, saith the Lord God.

And I will cause you to pass under the rod, and I will bring you into the bond of the covenant:

And I will purge out from among you the rebels, and them that transgress against me: I will bring them forth out of the country where they sojourn, and they shall not enter into the land of Israel: and ye shall know that I am the Lord. Ezekiel 20:33-38

Send ye the lamb to the ruler of the land from Sela to the wilderness, unto the mount of the daughter of Zion.

For it shall be, that, as a wandering bird cast out of the nest, so the daughters of Moab shall be at the fords of Amon.

Take counsel, execute judgment; make thy shadow as the night in the midst of the noonday; hide the outcasts; bewray not him that wandereth.

Let mine outcasts dwell with thee, Moab; be thou a covert to them from the face of the spoiler: for the extortioner is at an end, the spoiler ceaseth, the oppressors are consumed out of the land.

And in mercy shall the throne be established: and he shall sit upon it in truth in the tabernacle of David, judging, and seeking judgment, and hasting righteousness. Isaiah 16:1-5

Seventy weeks are determined upon thy people and upon thy holy city, to finish the transgression, and to make reconciliation for iniquity, and to bring in everlasting righteousness, and to seal up the vision and prophecy, and to anoint the most Holy.   Daniel 9:24

Therefore, behold, I will allure her, and bring her into the wilderness, and speak comfortably unto her.

And I will give her vineyards from thence, and the valley of Achor for a door of hope: and she shall sing there, as in the days of her youth, and as in the day when she came up out of the land of Egypt.

And it shall be at that day, saith the Lord, that thou shalt call me Ishi; and shalt call me no more Baali.

For I will take away the names of Baalim out of her mouth, and they shall no more be remembered by their name.

And in that day will I make a covenant for them with the beasts of the field, and with the fowls of heaven, and with the creeping things of the ground: and I will break the bow and the sword and the battle out of the earth, and will make them to lie down safely.

And I will betroth thee unto me for ever; yea, I will betroth thee unto me in righteousness, and in judgment, and in lovingkindness, and in mercies.

I will even betroth thee unto me in faithfulness: and thou shalt know the Lord.   Hosea 2:14-20

And the woman fled into the wilderness, where she hath a place prepared of God, that they should feed her there a thousand two hundred and threescore days.

And when the dragon saw that he was cast unto the earth, he persecuted the woman which brought forth the man child.

And to the woman were given two wings of a great eagle, that she might fly into the wilderness, into her place, where she is nourished for a time, and times, and half a time, from the face of the serpent.

And the serpent cast out of his mouth water as a flood

after the woman, that he might cause her to be carried away of the flood.

And the earth helped the woman, and the earth opened her mouth, and swallowed up the flood which the dragon cast out of his mouth.   Revelation 12:6,13-16

And Jesus answered and said unto them, Take heed that no man deceive you.

For many shall come in my name, saying, I am Christ; and shall deceive many.

And ye shall hear of wars and rumours of wars: see that ye be not troubled: for all these things must come to pass, but the end is not yet.

For nation shall rise against nation, and kingdom against kingdom: and there shall be famines, and pestilences, and earthquakes, in divers places.

All these are the beginning of sorrows.

Then shall they deliver you up to be afflicted, and shall kill you: and ye shall be hated of all nations for my name's sake.

And then shall many be offended, and shall betray one another, and shall hate one another.

And many false prophets shall rise, and shall deceive many.

And because iniquity shall abound, the love of many shall wax cold.

But he that shall endure unto the end, the same shall be saved.

And this gospel of the kingdom shall be preached in all the world for a witness unto all nations; and then shall the end come.

When ye therefore shall see the abomination of desolation, spoken of by Daniel the prophet, stand in the holy place, (whoso readeth, let him understand:)

Then let them which be in Judaea flee into the mountains:

Let him which is on the housetop not come down to take anything out of his house:

Neither let him which is in the field return back to take his clothes.

And woe unto them that are with child, and to them that give suck in those days!

But pray ye that your flight be not in the winter, neither on the sabbath day:

For then shall be great tribulation, such as was not since the beginning of the world to this time, no, nor ever shall be. Matthew 24:4-21

(3) During the seven year tribulation period, the antichrist will make himself known.

And after threescore and two weeks shall Messiah be cut off, but not for himself: and the people of the prince that shall come shall destroy the city and the sanctuary; and the end thereof shall be with a flood, and unto the end of the war desolations are determined.

And he shall confirm the covenant with many for one week: and in the midst of the week he shall cause the sacrifice and the oblation to cease, and for the overspreading of abominations he shall make it desolate, even until the consummation, and that determined shall be poured upon the desolate. Daniel 9:26, 27

When ye therefore shall see the abomination of desolation, spoken of by Daniel the prophet, stand in the holy place, (whoso readeth, let him understand:)

Matthew 24:15

But when ye shall see the abomination of desolation, spoken of by Daniel the prophet, standing where it ought not, (let him that readeth understand), then let them that be in Judaea flee to the mountains: Mark 13:14

Let no man deceive you by any means: for that day shall not come, except there come a falling away first, and that man of sin be revealed, the son of perdition;

Who opposeth and exalteth himself above all that is called God, or that is worshipped; so that he as God sitteth in the temple of God, shewing himself that he is God.

91

Remember ye not, that, when I was yet with you, I told you these things?

And now ye know what withholdeth that he might be revealed in his time.

For the mystery of iniquity doth already work: only he who now letteth will let, until he be taken out of the way.

And then shall that Wicked be revealed, whom the Lord shall consume with the spirit of his mouth, and shall destroy with the brightness of his coming:

Even him, whose coming is after the working of Satan with all power and signs and lying wonders,

And with all deceivableness of unrighteousness in them that perish; because they received not the love of the truth, that they might be saved.

And for this cause God shall send them strong delusion, that they should believe a lie:

That they all might be damned who believed not the truth, but had pleasure in unrighteousness.

II Thessalonians 2:3-12

(4) At the conclusion of the seven year tribulation, Christ will return all the way to the earth and defeat the antichrist and his armies.

*Enter into the rock, and hide thee in the **dust,** for fear of the Lord, and for the glory of **his** majesty.*

The lofty looks of man shall be humbled, and the haughtiness of men shall be bowed down, and the Lord alone shall be exalted in that day.

*For the day of the Lord of hosts shall be upon every one that is proud and lofty, and upon every one that is lifted up; and he shall **be** brought low:*

*And upon all the cedars of Lebanon, that **are** high and lifted up, and upon all the oaks of Bashan,*

And upon all the high mountains, and upon all the hills that are lifted up,

And upon every high tower, and upon every fenced wall,

And upon all the ships of Tarshish, and upon all pleasant pictures.

And the loftiness of man shall be bowed down, and the haughtiness of men shall be made low: and. the Lord alone shall be exalted in that day.

And the idols he shall utterly abolish.

And they shall go into the holes of the rocks, and into the caves of the earth, for fear of the Lord, and for the glory of his majesty, when he ariseth to shake terribly the earth.

In that day a man shall cast his idols of silver, and his idols of gold, which they made each one for himself to worship, to the moles and to the bats;

To go into the clefts of the rocks, and into the tops of the ragged rocks, for fear of the Lord, and for the glory of his majesty, when he ariseth to shake terribly the earth.

Isaiah 2:10-21

The word of the Lord came again unto me, saying,

Son of man, prophesy and say, Thus saith the Lord God; Howl ye. Woe worth the day!

For the day is near, even the day of the Lord is near, a cloudy day; it shall be the time of the heathen.

And the sword shall come upon Egypt, and great pain shall be in Ethiopia, when the slain shall fall in Egypt, and they shall take away her multitude, and her foundations shall be broken down.

Ethiopia, and Libya, and Lydia, and all the mingled people, and Chub, and the men of the land that is in league, shall fall with them by the sword.

Thus saith the Lord; They also that uphold Egypt shall fall; and the pride of her power shall come down: from the tower of Syene shall they fall in it by the sword, saith the Lord God.

And they shall be desolate in the midst of the countries that are desolate, and her cities shall be in the midst of the cities that are wasted.

And they shall know that I am the Lord, when I have set a fire in Egypt, and when all her helpers shall be destroyed.

Ezekiel 30:1-8

Alas for the day! for the day of the Lord is at hand, and as a destruction from the Almighty shall it come.

Joel 1:15

Assemble yourselves, and come, all ye heathen, and gather yourselves together round about: thither cause thy mighty ones to come down, 0 Lord.

Let the heathen be wakened, and come up to the valley of Jehoshaphat: for there will I sit to judge all the heathen round about.

Put ye in the sickle, for the harvest is ripe: come, get you down; for the press is full, the fats overflow; for their wickedness is great.

Multitudes, multitudes in the valley of decision: for the day of the Lord is near in the valley of decision.

The sun and the moon shall be darkened, and the stars shall withdraw their shining.

The Lord also shall roar out of Zion, and utter his voice from Jerusalem; and the heavens and the earth shall shake: but the Lord will be the hope of his people, and the strength of the children of Israel.

So shall ye know that I am the Lord your God dwelling in Zion, my holy mountain: then shall Jerusalem be holy, and there shall no strangers pass through her any more.

Joel 3:11-17

Hold thy peace at the presence of the Lord God: for the day of the Lord is at hand: for the Lord hath prepared a sacrifice, he hath prepared a sacrifice, he hath bid his guests.

And it shall come to pass in the day of the Lord's sacrifice, that I will punish the princes, and the king's children, and all such as are clothed with strange apparel.

Neither their silver nor their gold shall be able to deliver them in the day of the Lord's wrath; but the whole land shall be devoured by the fire of his jealousy: for he shall make even a speedy riddance of all them that dwell in the land.

Zephaniah 1:7, 8,18

Behold, the day of the Lord cometh, and thy spoil shall

be divided in the midst of thee.

For I will gather all nations against Jerusalem to battle: and the city shall be taken, and the houses rifled, and the women ravished; and half of the city shall go forth into captivity, and the residue of the people shall not be cut off from the city.

Then shall the Lord go forth, and fight against those nations, as when he fought in the day of battle.

Zechariah 14:1-3

But of the times and the seasons, brethren, ye have no need that I write unto you.

For yourselves know perfectly that the day of the Lord so cometh as a thief in the night.   I Thessalonians 5:1,2

And I saw heaven opened, and behold a white horse; and he that sat upon him was called Faithful and True, and in righteousness he doth judge and make war.

His eyes were as a flame of fire, and on his head were many crowns; and he had a name written, that no man knew, but he himself.

And he was clothed with a vesture dipped in blood: and his name is called The Word of God.

And the armies which were in heaven followed him upon white horses, clothed in fine linen, white and clean.

And out of his mouth goeth a sharp sword, that with it he should smite the nations: and he shall rule them with a rod of iron: and he treadeth the winepress of the fierceness of wrath of Almighty God.

And he hath on his vesture and on his thigh a name written, KING OF KINGS, AND LORD OF LORDS.

And I saw an angel standing in the sun; and he cried with a loud voice, saying to all the fowls that fly in the midst of heaven, Come and gather yourselves together unto the supper of the great God;

That ye may eat the flesh of kings, and the flesh of captains, and the flesh of mighty men, and the flesh of horses, and of them that sit on them, and the flesh of all men, both free and bond, both small and great.

And I saw the beast, and the kings of the earth, and their armies, gathered together to make war against him that sat on the horse, and against his army.

And the beast was taken, and with him the false prophet that wrought miracles before him, with which he deceived them that had received the mark of the beast, and them that worshipped his image. These both were cast alive into a lake of fire burning with brimstone.

And the remnant were slain with the sword of him that sat upon the horse, which sword proceeded out of his mouth: and all the fowls were filled with their flesh.

Revelation 19:11-21

(5) When the battle of Armageddon is over, at the conclusion of the seven year tribulation period, Christ will set up His earthly kingdom, and rule over it for one thousand years, without the presence of the devil, or Satan.

And it shall come to pass in that day, that the Lord shall punish the host of the high ones that are on high, and the kings of the earth upon the earth.

And they shall be gathered together, as prisoners are gathered in the pit, and shall be shut up in the prison, and after many days shall they be visited.

Then the moon shall be confounded, and the sun ashamed, when the Lord of hosts shall reign in mount Zion, and in Jerusalem, and before his ancients gloriously.

Isaiah 24:21-23

In that day the Lord with his sore and great and strong sword shall punish leviathan the piercing serpent, even leviathan that crooked serpent; and he shall slay the dragon that is in the sea.

Isaiah 27:1

And I saw an angel come down from heaven, having the key of the bottomless pit and a great chain in his hand.

And he laid hold on the dragon, that old serpent, which is the Devil, and Satan, and bound him a thousand years.

And cast him into the bottomless pit, and shut him up, and set a seal upon him, that he should deceive the na-

tions no more, till the thousand years should be fulfilled: and after that he must be loosed a little season.

And I saw thrones, and they sat upon them, and judgment was given unto them: and I saw the souls of them that were beheaded for the witness of Jesus, and for the word of God, and which had not worshipped the beast, neither his image, neither had received his mark upon their foreheads, or in their hands; and they lived and reigned with Christ a thousand years.

Revelation 20:1-4

In that day shall the branch of the Lord be beautiful and glorious, and the fruit of the earth shall be excellent and comely for them that are escaped of Israel.

And it shall come to pass, that he that is left in Zion, and he that remaineth in Jerusalem, shall be called holy, even every one that is written among the living in Jerusalem:

When the Lord shall have washed away the filth of the daughters of Zion, and shall have purged the blood of Jerusalem from the midst thereof by the spirit of judgement, and by the spirit of burning.

And the Lord will create upon every dwelling place of mount Zion, and upon her assemblies, a cloud and smoke by day, and the shining of a flaming fire by night: for upon all the glory shall be a defence.

And there shall be a tabernacle for a shadow in the daytime from the heat, and for a place of refuge, and for a covert from storm and from rain.   Isaiah 4:2-6

The wilderness and the solitary place shall be glad for them; and the desert shall rejoice, and blossom as the rose.

It shall blossom abundantly, and rejoice even with joy and singing: the glory of Lebanon shall be given unto it, the excellency of Carmel and Sharon, they shall see the glory of the Lord, and the excellency of our God.

Strengthen ye the weak hands, and confirm the feeble knees.

Say to them that are of a fearful heart, Be strong, fear

not: behold, your God will come with vengeance, even God with a recompence; he will come and save you.

Then the eyes of the blind shall be opened, and the ears of the deaf shall be unstopped.

Then shall the lame man leap as an hart, and the tongue of the dumb sing: for in the wilderness shall waters break out, and streams in the desert.

And the parched ground shall become a pool, and the thirsty land springs of water: in the habitation of dragons, where each lay, shall be grass with reeds and rushes.

And an highway shall be there, and a way, and it shall be called The way of holiness; the unclean shall not pass over it; but it shall be for those: the wayfaring men, though fools, shall not err therein.

No lion shall be there, not any ravenous beast shall go up thereon, it shall not be found there; but the redeemed shall walk there:

And the ransomed of the Lord shall return, and come to Zion with songs and everlasting Joy upon their heads: they shall obtain joy and gladness, and sorrow and sighing shall flee away.   Isaiah 35:1-10

(6) At the conclusion of the millennium (one thousand year reign of Christ), there will be one final battle. The devil will be destroyed by God Himself and the new heavens and the new earth will begin.

And when the thousand years are expired, Satan shall be loosed out of his prison,

And shall go out to deceive the nations which are in the four quarters of the earth, Gog and Magog, to gather them together to battle: the number of whom is as the sand of the sea.

And they went up on the breadth of the earth, and compassed the camp of the saints about, and the beloved city: and fire came down from God out of heaven, and devoured them.

And the devil that deceived them was cast into the lake of fire and brimstone, where the beast and the false prophet are, and shall be tormented day and night for ever and ever.

And I saw a great white throne, and him that sat on it, from whose face the earth and the heaven fled away; and there was found no place for them.

And I saw the dead, small and great, stand before God; and the books were opened: and another book was opened, which is the book of life: and the dead were judged out of those things which were written in the books, according to their works.

And the sea gave up the dead which were in it; and death and hell delivered up the dead which were in them: and they were judged every man according to their works.

And death and hell were cast into the lake of fire. This is the second death.

And whosoever was not found written in the book of life was cast into the lake of fire.   Revelation 20:7-15

And I saw a new heaven and a new earth: for the first heaven and the first earth were passed away; and there was no more sea.

And I John saw the holy city, new Jerusalem, coming down from God out of heaven, prepared as a bride adorned for her husband.

And I heard a great voice out of heaven saying, Behold, the tabernacle of God is with men, and he will dwell with them, and they shall be his people, and God himself shall be with them, and be their God.

And God shall wipe away all tears from their eyes; and there shall be no more death, neither sorrow, nor crying, neither shall there be any more pain: for the former things are passed away.

And he that sat upon the throne said, Behold, I make all things new. And he said unto me, Write: for these words are true and faithful.

And he said unto me, It is done. I am Alpha and Omega, the beginning and the end. I will give unto him that is athirst of the fountain of the water of life freely.

He that overcometh shall inherit all things; and I will be his God, and he shall be my son.   Revelation 21:1-7

A more complete description of the New Jerusalem can be found by reading all of Chapter 21 and 22 of Revelation.

I have no quarrel with those who have these events happening in a different sequence (even though I believe they are wrong).

One thing that needs to be understood, however, is that we must be saved, redeemed, born again, or whatever your terminology is for belonging to Christ.

Another, is that we must be overcomers, living a life of holiness.

Jesus answered and said unto him, Verily, verily, I say unto thee, Except a man be born again, he cannot see the kingdom of God.

For God so loved the world, that he gave his only begotten Son, that whosoever believeth in him should not perish, but have everlasting life.

For God sent not his Son into the world to condemn the world; but that the world through him might be saved.

He that believeth on him is not condemned: but he that believeth not is condemned already, because he hath not believed in the name of the only begotten Son of God.

John 3:3,16-18

What shall we say then? Shall we continue in sin, that grace may abound?

God forbid. How shall we, that are dead to sin, live any longer therein?   Romans 6:1-2

Giving thanks unto the Father, which hath made us meet to be partakers of the inheritance of the saints in light:

Who hath delivered us from the power of darkness, and hath translated us into the kingdom of his dear Son:

In whom we have redemption through his blood, even the forgiveness of sins: Colossians 1:12-14

If ye then be risen with Christ, seek those things which

are above, where Christ sitteth on the right hand of God.

Set your affection on things above, not on things on the earth. Colossians 3:1, 2

Wherefore lift up the hands which hang down, and the feeble knees;

And make straight paths for your feet, lest that which is lame be turned out of the way; but let it rather be healed.

Follow peace with all men, and holiness, without which no man shall see the Lord;

Looking diligently lest any man fail of the grace of God; lest any root of bitterness springing up trouble you, and thereby many be defiled; Hebrews 12:12-15

But if we walk in the light, as he is in the light, we have fellowship one with another, and the blood of Jesus Christ his Son cleanseth us from all sin. I John 1:7

Love not the world, neither the things that are in the world. If any man love the world, the love of the Father is not in him.

For all that is in the world, the lust of the flesh, and the lust of the eyes, and the pride of life, is not of the Father, but is of the world.

And world passeth away, and the lust thereof: but he that doeth the will of God abideth for ever. I John 2:15-17

To those who believe the seven year tribulation is a time of second chance for those who knew the truth of God's word but refused to live close enough to God to make the rapture, let me point out two things:

(1) Some believe no matter how careless they have lived, they can make heaven by refusing the mark of the beast. Most of the people I know cannot live two or three days without a cigarette, a cup of coffee, or fast even one day, let alone give up everything to keep from taking the mark of the beast.

And he causeth all, both small and great, rich and poor, free and bond, to receive a mark in their right hand, or in their foreheads:

And that no man might buy or sell, save he that had the

mark, or the name of the beast, or the number of his name.

Here is wisdom. Let him that hath understanding count the number of a man; and his number is Six hundred threescore and six.   Revelation 13:16-18

And the third angel followed them, saying with a loud voice. If any man worship the beast and his image, and receive his mark in his forehead, or in his hand,

The same shall drink of the wine of the wrath of God, which is poured out without mixture into the cup of his indignation; and he shall be tormented with fire and brimstone in the presence of the holy angels, and in the presence of the Lamb:

And the smoke of their torment ascendeth up for ever and ever: and they have no rest day nor night, who worship the beast and his image, and whosoever receiveth the mark of his name.   Revelation 14:9-11

(2) The scripture plainly teaches that those who refuse the truth before, will not want the truth when the antichrist is revealed.

And then shall that Wicked be revealed, whom the Lord shall consume with the spirit of his mouth, and shall destroy with the brightness of his coming:

Even him, whose coming is after the working of Satan with all power and signs and lying wonders,

And with all deceivableness of unrighteousness in them that perish; because they received not the love of the truth, that they might be saved.

And for this cause God shall send them strong delusion, that they should believe a lie:

That they all might be damned who believed not the truth, but had pleasure in unrighteousness.

II Thessalonians 2:8-12

Yes, there is a great future ahead for those who are serious about serving God.

As we said before, so say I now again. If any man preach any other gospel unto you than that ye have received, let him be accursed.   Galatians 1:9

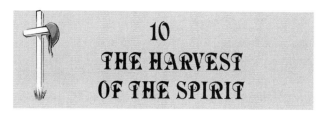

10
THE HARVEST
OF THE SPIRIT

*But the fruit of the Spirit is love, joy, peace, longsuffer-
ing, gentleness, goodness, faith,*
  Meekness, temperance: against such there is no law.
                                          Galatians 5:22, 23
  The fruit of the Spirit seems to be yet another subject
that has been entrusted to Paul to reveal to the body of
Christ.
  Moffatt, Weymouth, and some others translate Galatians
5:22 "the harvest of the Spirit is love, joy, peace," etc.
  The word **fruit** in Galatians 5:22, is taken from the
Greek word **karpos** which means "harvested, or plucked,
fruit."
  When we speak of the fruit, or harvest, of the Spirit, we
are speaking of the harvest brought forth by the Holy
Spirit in the believers life.
  No wonder Paul writes that "Against such there is no
law." How can there be? What fault can be found with
joy, or peace, or longsuffering? The Christian that mani-
fests in his life these nine fold graces is a joy to others, to
himself, and to God. This is spiritual maturity.
  The contrast with the fruit of the Spirit is the **works** of
the flesh. Fruit and "works" —the peace and freshness of
the orchard contrasted with the din and smoke and fever
of a factory, and worse. There is nothing beautiful about
the works of the flesh. They constitute a hideous list of
sinful passions, of satisfaction sought in unlawful ways
and never found, of feverish lust and brutal selfishness.
There is a "harvest" indeed of sowing to the flesh. "We
reap," says the Apostle, "corruption." Instead of the joy of
harvest, there is disillusionment and vanity. But from
sowing to the Spirit we shall reap life everlasting.[1]
  Before we thoroughly discuss the nine fruit of the Spirit,

let us identify the 17 works of the flesh Paul writes about as a background.

Now the works of flesh are manifest, which are these; Adultery, fornication, uncleanness, lasciviousness,

Idolatry, witchcraft, hatred, variance, emulations, wrath, strife, seditions, heresies,

Envyings, murders, drunkenness, revellings, and such like: of the which I tell you before, as I have also told you in time past, that they which do such things shall not inherit the kingdom of God. Galatians 5:19-21

I will briefly describe these works of the flesh.

ADULTERY:
Unlawful sexual relations between men and women.

FORNICATION:
The same as adultery, but including other unlawful relations. Many believe fornication is the same as adultery, only it is between the unmarried.

UNCLEANNESS:
The opposite of cleanness. The opposite of purity. Uncleanness can include all forms of sexual perversion.

LASCIVIOUSNESS:
That which promotes lewd emotions and encourages sin and lust.

IDOLATRY:
Can be anything that comes between us and God, or hinders our worship and service of God.

WITCHCRAFT:
Sorcery, enchantments, casting spells,
and the using of mind affecting drugs.

HATRED:
Bitterness, dislike, malice, grudges and
intense anger.

VARIANCE:
Quarreling, strife and discord.

EMULATIONS:
Fierce rivalry and intense struggling to best another.

WRATH:

Rage, fierce and lasting anger.

STRIFE:
Arguing, disputing, endeavoring to pay back for real or imaginary wrongs.

SEDITIONS:
Stirring up strife and establishing factions in homes, governments, churches, etc.

HERESIES:
Heresies are a lot like seditions, disunions, disorderly, a party of factional spirit.

ENVYINGS:
Being jealous over someone's good fortune and blessing.

MURDERS:
To kill or destroy another.

DRUNKENNESS:
Being intoxicated by drink.

REVELLINGS:
Lascivious and noisy parties, many times with obscene music and drunkenness.

After describing the 17 works of the flesh, we can readily see the beauty of the fruit of the Spirit, and once again emphasize that it is no wonder Paul concludes describing the fruit with the words "Against such there is no law."

In seeking now to deal with the nine fruit of the Spirit listed in Galatians 5:22-23, I am proposing a quite arbitrary division which I trust will be helpful nevertheless. I suggest dividing them into three groups of three in this way: (1) a harvest for others;(2) a harvest for ourselves; (3) a harvest for God.

To forestall possible objections, may I say at once that this grouping is purely a matter of convenience for study. All nine fruit of the Spirit provide equally a harvest of happiness for others, for ourselves, and for God. Particularly is it true that all nine bring glory to God.

Arising from this, it is proper to emphasize that if we use the term "fruit" of the Spirit, as in the A. V., we should note that it is a single collective noun: it is not "fruits."

There should be no question of picking and choosing between the different qualities of character. They constitute the whole, and are to be regarded collectively as the proper result of a believers walking in the Spirit.

This important aspect of the truth is made more clear if we use the term "harvest" rather than "fruit" of the Spirit. Taken together they present a full-orbed manifestation of the character of a man in Christ Jesus.[2]

I. A HARVEST FOR OTHERS
LOVE:

The fruit of **love** mentioned in Galatians 5:22 is taken from the same word **agape** as is the word **charity** in I Corinthians 13:1.

This love is a divine love which is tender while at the same time ardent and strong. It is a love devoted to the well being of others.

This is the love whereby we are able to carry out Christ's command to "love your enemies."

Ye have heard that it hath been said, Thou shalt love thy neighbour, and hate thine enemy.

But I say unto you. Love your enemies, bless them that curse you, do good to them that hate you, and pray for them which despitefully use you, and persecute you;

That ye may be the children of your Father which is in heaven: for he maketh his sun to rise on the evil and on the good, and sendeth rain on the just and on the unjust.

For if ye love them which love you, what reward have ye? do not even the publicans the same?

And if ye salute your brethren only, what do ye more than others? do not even the publicans so?

Be ye therefore perfect, even as your Father which is in heaven is perfect.   Matthew 5:43-48

This agape love enables us to love the unlovely. Some individuals are difficult to love.

Missionaries, pastors, and social workers need the harvest of the Spirit called love, to enable them to carry out their duties. This love enables the maximum benefit to flow to the recipient.

I believe it was this love which enabled John, originally referred to as one of the "Sons of Thunder," to become known as "the apostle of love." The one whom legend tells us, when he was so old he could no longer preach, would say to the departing congregation, "little children, love one another."

Beloved, let us love one another: for love is of God; and every one that loveth is born of God, and knoweth God.

I John 4:7

LONGSUFFERING:

The ability to patiently bear long with the faults and frailties of others, without murmuring and resentment.

The true fruit of the Spirit is victorious and voluntary. It suffers with a grin. Indeed, it can so cleverly conceal itself that onlookers mistakenly imagine that the one in view has nothing to worry about, and no particular test for patience. That is victory.[3]

To be longsuffering is to be God-like. If it were not for the longsuffering of the Heavenly Father, mankind would have been annihilated long ago.

GENTLENESS:

To have a kind, gentle, soft spoken, even-tempered manner.

Some Bible translators have translated the word **gentleness** to read **kindness.** Gentleness can often be misunderstood to be weakness. Not so! It requires great strength to be truly gentle.

Several years ago I was on board the Queen Mary on one occasion when she arrived at New York. There was some kind of strike on, and the usual tugs were not available to bring the huge boat up to the dock. But with consummate skill the pilot brought the vessel in, a foot at a time, until at last we touched the dock with gentleness. No other word describes the achievement so well. All the immense power of the engines that had brought us swiftly across the Atlantic was under such perfect control, and the steering equipment responded so perfectly to the touch, that it added up to a superb piece of navigation. It illustrated what I have always felt to be the finest definition of gentleness— "power under perfect control." Any lack of gentleness would have been disastrous.[4]

Jesus, our perfect example, is said to **have** welcomed the little children to fellowship with Him. Lesser, weaker personalities would have scattered the children and sent them away. Strength is required to be gentle. Often it is the insecure individual who boasts and talks loudly of his accomplishments.

David, after his battle with Goliath, did not need to wear a badge or button proclaiming his greatness. David's greatness was evident for all to see.

It is usually the fearful one who whistles loudly while walking past the cemetery on a dark night. One with courage can well afford to hold his peace.

It is God that girdeth me with strength, and maketh my way perfect.

He maketh my feet like hinds feet, and setteth me upon my high places.

He teacheth my hands to war, so that a bow of steel is broken by mine arms.

Thou hast also given me the shield of thy salvation: and thy right hand hath holden me up, and thy gentleness hath made me great.   Psalm 18:32-35

II. A HARVEST FOR OURSELVES
JOY:

This joy Paul mentions here is not some earthly joy or gladness which any heathen might possess.

It is not even dependent on what **happens** to us, as some have described **happiness.**

This joy is a fruit, a divine possession which abides when our hearts seem to be breaking. Like the **apple** hangs on the **apple tree** even when the weather is stormy, and the sun shines not, this joy is a fruit that is evident in the true Christian.

This joy comes not from everything going well for us, but rather it comes from abiding in the presence of God.

Thou wilt shew me the path of life: in thy presence is fulness of joy; at thy right hand there are pleasures for evermore. Psalm 16:11

I have seen this joy manifest itself at the most unexpected time, even to the surprise of the one possessing it. In the darkest hour there is sometimes a holy laughter that emanates from its possessor.

This joy enables us to overcome almost impossible circumstances.

...for the joy of the Lord is your strength.

Nehemiah 8:10

Looking unto Jesus the author and finisher of our faith; who for the joy that was set before him endured the cross, despising the shame, and is set down at the right hand of the throne of God. Hebrews 12:2

Joy comes from abiding in, and obeying the commandments of, our Lord Jesus Christ.

As the Father hath loved me, so have I loved you: continue ye in my love.

If ye keep my commandments, ye shall abide in my love; even as I have kept my Father's commandments, and abide in his love.

These things have I spoken unto you, that my joy might remain in you, and that your joy might be full.

John 15:9-11

This joy is an excitement, a gladness and a delight, that enables us to have a deep settled peace and satisfaction.

PEACE:

The state of quiet rest, repose and harmony with God and His plan for our lives.

There is no peace, saith my God, to the wicked.

Isaiah 57:21

Peace I leave with you, my peace I give unto you: not as

the world giveth, give I unto you. Let not your heart be
troubled, neither let it be afraid.   John 14:27

Governments are said to be at peace when there is an absence of a declared war.

Marriages are presumed to be at peace when they are in the state of cold war.

But this peace, this harvest of the Spirit is much more than a mere absence of fighting.

This peace defies human reasoning. We sometimes find ourselves **getting worried** that we are not **getting worried.**

Paul says:

Be careful (anxious) *for nothing; but in every thing by*
prayer and supplication with thanksgiving let your re-
quests be made known unto God.

And the peace of God, which passeth all understanding,
shall keep your hearts and miinds through Christ Jesus.
                                        Philippians 4:6, 7

And there we seem to have it, "which passeth (goes beyond) all understanding."

This peace adds an entire new dimension to the life of its possessor.

TEMPERANCE:

I think temperance can be easily defined as self-control. It is truly being in control of self. With temperance, we can live a life of moderation.

Let your moderation be known unto all men. The Lord is
at hand.   Philippians 4:5

Know ye not that they which run in a race run all, but
one receiveth the prize? So run, that ye may obtain.

And every man that striveth for the mastery is temperate
in all things. Now they do it to obtain a corruptible
crown; but we an incorruptible.

I therefore so run, not as uncertainly; so fight I, not as
one that beateth the air:

But I keep under my body, and bring it into subjection:

lest that by any means, when I have preached to others, I myself should be a castaway.   I Corinthians 9:24-27

One of the saddest facts in connection with successful evangelists is the number that fall through physical sins. It is possible that Satan uses their very success in evangelism to lull them into a false sense of security."

It is in self-control of the body that fasting finds its proper place.

The great value of fasting is in maintaining control over bodily appetites. The body is to be our servant, and not our master.[5]

We talk of temperance mostly in the physical realm, but we need temperance in the spirit and soul as well.

III. A HARVEST FOR GOD
GOODNESS:

The state of being good. To be God-like in character, life, and conduct.

There are people who manifest this attribute, and you just feel good for having known them.

A *good man out of the good treasure of the heart bringeth forth good things: and an evil man out of the evil treasure bringeth forth evil things.*   Matthew 12:35

Cleverness has enabled many a man to "get by" for a time, but eventually any failure in goodness of character will manifest itself.

Jesus said in Mark 9:50, "Salt is good..."

Jesus also described his followers this way:

Ye are the salt of the earth: but if the salt have lost his savour, wherewith shall it be salted? it is thenceforth good for nothing, but to be cast out, and to be trodden under foot of men.   Matthew 5:13

We are to be good, to be salt. We are to be a preserving, stabilizing influence in our world.

That ye might walk worthy of the Lord unto all pleasing, being fruitful in every good work, and increasing in the knowledge of God;   Colossians 1:10

Goodness is the part of the harvest of the Spirit upon which all ministries and gifts of the Holy Spirit can safely be built.

FAITH:

Some Bible scholars believe the word **faith** in Galatians 5:22 should have been translated faithfulness, or fidelity.

God is absolutely trustworthy, or faithful. If we desire to be like God, we must learn faithfulness.

Know therefore that the Lord thy God, he is God, the faithful God, which keepeth covenant and mercy with them that love him and keep his commandments to a thousand generations; Deuteronomy 7:9

If we believe not, yet he abideth faithful: he cannot deny himself. II Timothy 2:13

Wherefore let them that suffer according to the will of God commit the keeping of their souls to him in well do-ing, as unto a faithful Creator. I Peter 4:19

Any stable society must be founded upon faithfulness. The conduct of business could ultimately become impos-sible if men were not faithful in their commercial deal-ings with one another. That is why a good name in the business world is such a vital asset. An unfaithful busi-ness firm, or bank, or manufacturer, or professional man soon heads for bankruptcy in disgrace. Customers have to be faithful for their credit to be good.

Home life is founded on faithfulness to the marriage vows made by a husband and wife. We call adultery "unfaithfulness," and so it is. The foundations of any civi-lization shows sinister cracks when marriage vows are taken lightly. Stable home life is made impossible, and so the unit of national life is almost destroyed. To be faithful is more important than to be "happy," although normally the two go together.[6]

We have learned to love and admire those faithful he-roes of the Bible. Heroes, who could not have been he-roes, had they not been found faithful.

Fear none of those things which thou shall suffer: be-

hold, the devil shall cast some of you into prison, that ye may be tried; and ye shall have tribulation ten days: be thou faithful unto death, and I will give thee a crown of life.   Revelation 2:10

At some point in our Christian growth, we must determine that whether or not we ever become great, one thing we all can do is to be faithful.

MEEKNESS:

To be patient in suffering injuries without feeling a spirit of revenge. To have a kind balanced disposition.

But let it be the hidden man of the heart, in that which is not corruptible, even the ornament of a meek and quiet spirit, which is in the sight of God of great price.
                                                    I Peter 3:4

The fruit, or harvest, of meekness is probably one of the lesser desired by us, but one of the most important to God.

Brethren, if a man be overtaken in a fault, ye which are spiritual, restore such an one in the spirit of meekness; considering thyself, lest thou also be tempted.
                                                    Galatians 6:1

Take my yoke upon you, and learn of me; for I am meek and lowly in heart: and ye shall find rest unto your souls.
                                                    Matthew 11:29

Tell ye the daughter of Sion, Behold, thy King cometh unto thee, meek...   Matthew 21:5

We have Bible examples of very strong men who were also very meek men.

(Now the man Moses was very meek, above all the men which were upon the face of the earth.)   Numbers 12:3

Then said Abishai the son of Zeruiah unto the king, Why should this dead dog curse my lord the king? let me go over, I pray thee, and take off his head.

And the king said, What have I to do with you, ye sons of Zeruiah? so let him curse, because the Lord hath said unto him, Curse David. Who shall then say, Wherefore has thou done so?

And David said to Abishai, and to all his servants, Behold, my son, which came forth of my bowels, seeketh my life: how much more now may this Benjamite do it? let him alone, and let him curse; for the Lord hath bidden him. II Samuel 16:9-11

Meekness is a must in those who would be servants of God.

And the servant of the Lord must not strive; but be gentle unto all men, apt to teach, patient,

In meekness instructing those that oppose themselves; if God peradventure will give them repentance to the acknowledging of the truth; II Timothy 2:24, 25

Meekness is surrendering our will, willingly, to a greater will than our own.

We must keep in mind that to please God we must bear fruit.

Herein is my Father glorified, that ye bear much fruit; so shall ye be my disciples. John 15:8

As we said before, so say I now again, If any man preach any other gospel unto you than that ye have received, let him be accursed. Galatians 1:9

1. Donald Gee, **Fruitful or Barren,** Gospel Publishing House, Springfield, Missouri, 1961, page 2.

2. Ibid., page 14.

3. Ibid., page 22.

4. Ibid., page 26.

5. Ibid., page 46, 47.

6. Ibid., page 58.

11
GRACE

The word **GRACE** is used in the writings of Paul no less than 89 times, 97 if you attribute the Book of Hebrews to Paul.

Counting the Book of Hebrews to have been written by someone other than Paul, the word **GRACE** is used only 78 times in the entire Bible, outside of Paul's writings.

So here is another subject the Apostle Paul appears to be eminently qualified to discuss.

What does the word **GRACE** really mean, and how far do the repercussions of **GRACE** go?

The word in Hebrew used all but one time to refer to **GRACE** in the Old Testament is **chen,** pronounced khane, and means "favor, grace, pleasant, precious, (well) favored."

The only word in Greek that is translated to read **GRACE,** all but one time, is **charis,** pronounced khar'-ece, and means "acceptable, benefit, favor, gift, grace (-ious), joy, liberality, pleasures, thank(-s,—worthy)."

It is important to note that there are false theories of grace being taught. There is a school of interpreters who magnify the grace of God above all else in the program of God. They ignore God's justice, laws, and all conditions regulating and governing the grace of God in the lives of mankind.

While grace is an extremely important aspect in the dealings of God with free moral agents, grace is not the sum total of all there is to know about God, His plan, and His dealings with man.

It seems that some are bent on the exalting of grace to the point of excluding man's responsibility.

As I stated in another book, that old hackneyed expression, "Thank God we are not under law: we're under grace!" has come to mean something entirely different from that which God intended.

Consider the following:

And the Lord said, I will destroy man whom I have created from the face of the earth; both man, and beast, and the creeping thing, and the fowls of the air; for it repenteth me that I have made them.

But Noah found grace in the eyes of the Lord.

Genesis 6:7, 8

It would be easy to lift that scripture out of its context and use the definition of grace that has become so popular in our time, namely, that grace is "unmerited favor." However, let us look at the following verse.

These are the generations of Noah: Noah was a just man and perfect in his generations, and Noah walked with God.

Genesis 6:9

It soon becomes obvious why Noah found grace in the eyes of the Lord. Noah walked with God. Let's face it, none of us, in ourselves, deserve the grace of God. For even when we obey God, and walk as close to perfection as we possibly can, the truth is we are doing even that because of the grace of God in our lives.

I have wondered many times why I was born into a Christian home rather than in the home of some devil worshiper somewhere.

Why is it that I am saved and know Christ in an intimate way when many of my neighbors not only do not know Him, they are not even interested in knowing Him.

The answer surely must be, grace. When we sing that lovely hymn "GRACE GREATER THAN ALL OUR SINS," it must surely humble us to know that God saved us, not because we were good, but because He is good.

And yet, if everything depended only upon God to save every sinner, and they had nothing to do to get saved, than all would be saved by God. If everything were left up to God, then He would be under moral obligation to save everyone, regardless of their consent, or He would be a respecter of persons.

116

Let us realize that grace is favor, unmerited favor if you will, but grace has a price tag attached to it. Grace leaves **us** with obligations to fulfill.

For grace to be effective, the recipient must respond and show his responsibility.

Let us look to the Apostle of Grace, Paul, for instruction.

What shall we say then? Shall we continue in sin, that grace may abound?

God forbid. How shall we, that are dead to sin, live any longer therein?

Let not sin reign in your mortal body, that ye should obey it in the lusts thereof.

For sin shall not have dominion over you: for ye are not under the law, but under grace.   Romans 6:1, 2,12,14

Grace does not ignore man's responsibility, it magnifies it.

The word **grace** is used repeatedly to refer to the manifestation of the favor of God to man, and this favor is governed by the disposition, life, service, faith, and attitude of the recipient of the favor.

For the grace of God that bringeth salvation hath appeared to all men,

Teaching us that, denying ungodliness and worldly lusts, we should live soberly, righteously, and godly, in this present world;

Looking for that blessed hope, and the glorious appearing of the great God and our Saviour Jesus Christ;

Who gave himself for us, that he might redeem us from all iniquity, and purify unto himself a peculiar people, zealous of good works.   Titus 2:11-14

Many are willing to receive the grace that brings salvation, but they are unwilling to receive that grace that becomes the teacher.

Notice that Paul said in Titus 2:11 that the grace of God, that bringeth salvation hath appeared to **all** men. Now in order for that grace to become effective it must be received and acted upon.

When men in the early church found grace from God, it was because they humbled themselves and by their own choice accepted God's salvation.

On the other hand, when they failed God, they fell under the condemnation of God just as the Israelites and others. Notice these examples:

That he may take part of this ministry and apostleship, from which Judas by transgression fell, that he might go to his own place. Acts 1:25

But a certain man named Ananias, with Sapphira his wife, sold a possession,

And kept back part of the price, his wife also being privy to it, and brought a certain part, and laid it at the apostles' feet.

But Peter said, Ananias, why hath Satan filled thine heart to lie to the Holy Ghost, and to keep back part of the price of the land?

Whiles it remained, was it not thine own? and after it was sold, was it not in thine own power? why hast thou conceived this thing in thine heart? thou hast not lied unto men, but unto God.

And Ananias hearing these words fell down, and gave up the ghost: and great fear came on all them that heard these things. Acts 5:1-5

Holding faith, and a good conscience; which some having put away concerning faith have made shipwreck:

Of whom is Hymenaeus and Alexander; whom I have delivered unto Satan, that they may learn not to blaspheme. I Timothy 1:19, 20

For it is impossible for those who were once enlightened, and have tasted of the heavenly gift, and were made partakers of the Holy Ghost,

And have tasted the good word of God, and the powers of the world to come,

If they shall fall away, to renew them again unto repentance; seeing they crucify to themselves the Son of God afresh, and put Him to an open shame. Hebrews 6:4-6

For if we sin wilfully after that we have received the knowledge of the truth, there remaineth no more sacrifice for sins,

But a certain fearful looking for of judgement and fiery indignation, which shall devour the adversaries.

He that despised Moses' law died without mercy under two or three witnesses:

Of how much sorer punishment, suppose ye, shall he be thought worthy, who hath trodden underfoot the Son of God, and hath counted the blood of the covenant, wherewith he was sanctified, an unholy thing, and hath done despite unto the Spirit of grace?   Hebrews 10:26-29

For if after they have escaped the pollutions of the world through the knowledge of the Lord and Saviour Jesus Christ, they are again entangled therein, and overcome, the latter end is worse with them than the beginning.

For it had been better for them not to have known the way of righteousness, than, after they have known it, to turn from the holy commandment delivered unto them.

But it is happened unto them according to the true proverb. The dog is turned to his own vomit again; and the sow that was washed to her wallowing in the mire.

                    II Peter 2:20-22

Remember therefore from whence thou art fallen, and repent, and do the first works; or else I will come unto thee quickly, and will remove thy candlestick out of his place, except thou repent.   Revelation 2:5

To keep God's grace in our lives, it must be received with gladness and acted upon with responsibility.

There are things that grace cannot do.

Grace cannot excuse and ignore our failure to meet the condition of salvation.

There is therefore now no condemnation to them which are in Christ Jesus, who walk not after the flesh, but after the Spirit.

For the law of the Spirit of life in Christ Jesus hath made me free from the law of sin and death.

For what the law could not do, in that it was weak through the flesh, God sending his own Son in the likeness of sinful flesh, and for sin, condemned sin in the flesh:

That the righteousness of the law might be fulfilled in us, who walk not after the flesh, but after the Spirit.

For they that are after the flesh do mind the things of the flesh; but they that are after the Spirit the things, of the Spirit.

For to be carnally minded is death; but to be spiritually minded is life and peace.

Because the carnal mind is enmity against God: for it is not subject to the law of God, neither indeed can be.

So then they that are in the flesh cannot please God.

But ye are not in the flesh, but in the Spirit, if so be that the Spirit of God dwell in you. Now if any man have not the Spirit of Christ, he is none of his.

And if Christ be in you, the body is dead because of sin; but the Spirit is life because of righteousness.

But if the Spirit of him that raised up Jesus from the dead dwell in you, he that raised up Christ from the dead shall also quicken your mortal bodies by his Spirit that dwelleth in you.

Therefore, brethren, we are debtors, not to the flesh, to live after the flesh.

For if ye live after the flesh, ye shall die: but if ye through the Spirit do mortify the deeds of the body, ye shall live.   Romans 8:1-13

Notice how many times the Apostle Paul uses the word "if in the preceding verses.

Yes, grace extended God's hand of forgiveness when we did not deserve it.

But God commendeth his love toward us, in that, while we were yet sinners, Christ died for us.   Romans 5:8

But God's grace does not, and cannot, keep men saved when they insist on continuing on in their sins.

Paul, writing to the church at Corinth, gives us the following warning.

Know ye not that the unrighteous shall not inherit the

kingdom of God? Be not deceived: neither fornicators, nor idolaters, nor adulterers, nor effeminate, nor abusers of themselves with mankind,

Nor thieves, nor covetous, nor drunkard, nor revilers, nor extortioners shall inherit the kingdom of God.

I Corinthians 6:9,10

Again, Paul is writing to the church; this time to all the churches of Galatia.

Now the works of the flesh are manifest, which are these; Adultery, fornication, uncleanness, lasciviousness,

Idolatry, witchcraft, hatred, variance, emulations, wrath, strife, seditions, heresies. Galatians 5:19, 20

Grace cannot permit God to forgive the unrepentant person, be they believer or unbeliever.

Grace cannot be construed to imply that God is soft on sin.

Be not deceived; God is not mocked: for whatsoever a man soweth, that shall he also reap.

For he that soweth to his flesh shall of the flesh reap corruption; but he that soweth to the Spirit shall of the Spirit reap life everlasting. Galatians 6:7, 8

Let us rejoice, humbly, in that God has bestowed His grace upon us. Let us also recognize our responsibility to encourage grace to continue to work in our lives.

Then, when we are obeying God in every avenue of His dealings with us, yes, even when we are in the company of those who do not even try to live as close to God as we; the recognition of the force of grace in our lives, instead of causing us to be proud, will serve to humble us as we realize that were it not for God's grace — extended, received, and acted upon — we would still be a lost sinner.

As we said before, so say I now again, If any man preach any other gospel unto you than that ye have received, let him be accursed. Galatians 1:9

12
UNCONDITIONAL ETERNAL SECURITY

Can a saved person ever be lost?

Can a person to whom eternal life is given ever lose that eternal life?

One well-known, international evangelist made the statement, "When the rapture of the church takes place, God will call His people out of the taverns, and out of their beds of adultery, and take them home to heaven."

In answer to the question, "What if a person who has been saved, later decides that he or she does not want to go to heaven?" An internationally known radio evangelist wrote the following answer:

"If you are once saved, and you decide you do not want to go to heaven, even if you shake your fist at God in heaven, and curse Him to His face, you would be forced by God to go to heaven because you once were saved."

The two preceding statements are foolish to the extreme and are the result of trying to defend an erroneous doctrine.

Let's look at some of the scripture references given to attempt to prove unconditional eternal security.

Who shall separate us from the love of Christ? shall tribulation, or distress, or persecution, or famine, or nakedness, or peril, or sword?

As it is written, For thy sake we are killed all the day long; we are accounted as sheep for the slaughter.

Nay, in all these things we are more than conquerors through him that loved us.

For I am persuaded, that neither death, nor life, nor angels, nor principalities, nor powers, nor things present, nor things to come,

Nor height, nor depth, nor any other creature, shall be able to separate us from the love of God, which is in

Christ Jesus our Lord.   Romans 8:35-39

We will come back to this reference later, but I must say I am in complete agreement with Romans 8:35-39.

My sheep hear my voice, and I know them, and they follow me:

And I give unto them eternal life; and they shall never perish, neither shall any man pluck them out of my hand.

My Father, which gave them me, is greater than all; and no man is able to pluck them out of my Father's hand.

John 10:27-29

Again I say, I am in complete agreement with the preceding reference.

Many are being deceived by the doctrine of eternal security. They think that because they have been saved, they can go back into sin and still be saved. In the letters to the seven churches in Revelation, Chapters 2 and 3, we read continual warnings from Christ to repent. In addition to these warnings to repent, Christ makes it very plain that the promises of rewards are to the overcomer.

He that hath an ear, let him hear what the Spirit saith unto the churches; to him that overcometh will I give to eat of the tree of life, which is in the midst of the paradise of God.

He that hath an ear, let him hear what the Spirit saith unto the churches; He that overcometh shall not be hurt of the second death.

He that hath an ear, let him hear what the Spirit saith unto the churches; To him that overcometh will I give to eat of the hidden manna, and will give him a white stone, and in the stone a new name written, which no man knoweth saving he that receiveth it.

And he that overcometh, and keepeth my works unto the end, to him will I give power over the nations:

Revelation 2:7, 11, 17, 26

He that overcometh, the same shall be clothed in white raiment; and I will not blot out his name out of the book of life, but I will confess his name before my Father, and before his angels.

Him that overcometh will I make a pillar in the temple of my God, and he shall go no more out: and I will write upon him the name of my God, and the name of the city of my God, which is new Jerusalem, which cometh down out of heaven from my God: and I will write upon him my new name.

To him that overcometh will I grant to sit with me in my throne, even as I also overcame and am set down with my Father in his throne.   Revelation 3:5, 12, 21

Please notice that every promise of victory and reward is to the overcomer. This seems so foreign to today's church attenders who are told such things as, "Well, we all have to sin a little every day."

One young man was told at a church camp that every Christian sins at least three times every day.

Others are told, "Just do the best you can and God will take you to heaven, after all, we are under grace."

The Bible plainly teaches us that sin will not enter heaven. Listen again to the Apostle Paul.

That he might present it to himself a glorious church, not having spot, or wrinkle, or any such thing; but that it should be holy and without blemish.   Ephesians 5:27

Where do we get these ideas that we can just goof-off spiritually and God will accept us? These dangerous theories come from the dangerous doctrine called eternal security.

Going back to Romans 8:35-39, we find that the Apostle Paul tells us in no uncertain terms that, "...nothing can separate us from the love of God, which is in Christ Jesus."

So then, why the concern? Paul is giving us in these verses the precious truth that we are safe in Jesus Christ. Safe from anything in creation. But remember, we are free moral agents. Just as we can follow Christ, we can also decide to stop following Him.

For Demas hath forsaken me, having loved this present

124

world, and is departed unto Thessalonica...

II Timothy 4:10

Ye adulterers and adulteresses, know ye not that the friendship of the world is enmity with God? whosoever therefore will be a friend of the world is the enemy of God.

James 4:4

There was no dark power in this world that could take Demas back to the world of sin. He, himself, made the decision, willingly, deliberately.

Judas Iscariot did the same. To those who claim Judas Iscariot was never really a believer, let me give you the following scripture references.

And when he had called unto him his twelve disciples, he gave them power against unclean spirits, to cast them out, and to heal all manner of sickness and all manner of disease.

Now the names of the twelve apostles are these; The first, Simon, who is called Peter, and Andrew his brother; James the son of Zebedee, and John his brother;

Philip, and Bartholomew; Thomas, and Matthew the publican; James the son of Alphaeus, and Lebbaeus, whose surname was Thaddaeus;

Simon the Canaanite, and Judas Iscariot, who also betrayed him.

Matthew 10:1-4

I cannot help but believe Judas was originally a follower of Jesus Christ. He was given the same power as the eleven. He was counted an apostle. He was filled with the Holy Spirit.

And ye shall be brought before governors and kings for my sake, for a testimony against them and the Gentiles.

But when they deliver you up, take no thought how or what ye shall speak: for it shall be given you in that same hour what ye shall speak.

For it is not ye that speak, but the Spirit of your Father which speaketh in you.

Matthew 10:18-20

HE WAS ORDAINED TO PREACH:

And he ordained twelve, that they should be with him,

and that he might send them forth to preach.

And to have power to heal sicknesses, and to cast out devils:

And Judas Iscariot, which also betrayed him: and they went into an house. Mark 3:14, 15,19

HE WAS ENDUED WITH POWER:

And as ye go, preach, saying. The kingdom of heaven is at hand.

Heal the sick, cleanse the lepers, raise the dead, cast out devils: freely ye have received, freely give.

Matthew 10:7, 8

HE WAS TRUSTED TO BAPTIZE CONVERTS IN WATER:

When therefore the Lord knew how the Pharisees had heard that Jesus made and baptized more disciples than John,

(Though Jesus himself baptized not, but his disciples,)

John 4:1, 2

You may refer to the words of Jesus, in John 6:70 and 71, and say Judas was never saved. I believe the entire context of scripture concerning Judas proves that he was a saved man.

Jesus answered them, Have not I chosen you twelve, and one of you is a devil?

He spake of Judas Iscariot the son of Simon: for he it was that should betray him, being one of the twelve.

John 6:70, 71

Judas was a saved man, in fact, he was a bishop. His name was also in the book of life:

For it is written in the book of Psalms, Let his habitation be desolate, and let no man dwell therein: and his bishoprick let another take. Acts 1:20

The following scripture is quoted in Acts 1:20 concerning Judas.

Let their habitation be desolate; and let none dwell in their tents.

For they persecute him whom thou hast smitten; and they

talk to the grief of those whom thou hast wounded.

Add iniquity unto their iniquity: and let them not come into thy righteousness.

Let them be blotted out of the book of the living, and not be written with the righteous. Psalms 69:25-28

To believe a saved person can never be lost is to ignore important Bible teaching. Let us look at four individuals who do not believe saved people can never be lost.

GOD AND MOSES:

And it came to pass on the morrow, that Moses said unto the people. Ye have sinned a great sin: and now I will go up unto the Lord; peradventure I shall make an atonement for your sin.

And Moses returned unto the Lord, and said. Oh, this people have sinned a great sin, and have made them gods of gold.

Yet now, if thou wilt forgive their sin—and if not, blot me, I pray thee, out of thy book which thou hast written.

And the Lord said unto Moses, Whosoever hath sinned against me, him will I blot out of my book.

Exodus 32:30-33

DAVID:

Add iniquity unto their iniquity: and let them not come into thy righteousness.

Let them be blotted out of the book of the living, and not be written with the righteous. Psalm 69:27, 28

JESUS CHRIST:

He that overcometh, the same shall be clothed in white raiment; and I will not blot out his name out of the book of life, but I will confess his name before my Father, and before his angels. Revelation 3:5

And if any man shall take away from the words of the book of this prophecy, God shall take away his part out of the book of life, and out of the holy city, and from the things which are written in this book. Revelation 22:19

The word **blot** in all the preceding scriptures means, "abolish, destroy, smear out, erase or obliterate."

127

While there are scriptures that talk about blotting out names **under** heaven, the preceding scriptures definitely talk about blotting names **out of God's book of life.**

Can eternal life be taken away from a person to whom it has been given?

But Christ as a son over his own house; whose house are we, if we holdfast the confidence and the rejoicing of the hope firm unto the end. Hebrews 3:6

Follow peace with all men, and holiness, without which no man shall see the Lord: Hebrews 12:14

For it is impossible for those who were once enlightened, and have tasted of the heavenly gift, and were made partakers of the Holy Ghost,

And have tasted the good word of God, and the powers of the world to come,

If they shall fall away, to renew them again unto repentance; seeing they crucify to themselves the Son of God afresh, and put him to an open shame. Hebrews 6:4-6

For if we sin willfully after that we have received the knowledge of the truth, there remaineth no more sacrifice for sins,

But a certain fearful looking for of judgment and fiery indignation, which shall devour the adversaries.

He that despised Moses' law died without mercy under two or three witnesses:

Of how much sorer punishment, suppose ye, shall he be thought worthy, who hath trodden underfoot the Son of God, and hath counted the blood of the covenant, wherewith he was sanctified, an unholy thing, and hath done despite unto the Spirit of grace?

For we know him that hath said, Vengeance belongeth unto me, I will recompense, saith the Lord. And again, the Lord shall judge his people.

It is a fearful thing to fall into the hands of the living God. Hebrews 10:26-31

The entire promise of eternal life is based on continuing to follow Jesus Christ, and to grow in grace and truth.

Then said Jesus to those Jews which believed on him, If ye continue in my word, then are ye my disciples indeed;

John 8:31

Who are kept by the power of God through faith unto salvation ready to be revealed in the last time.

Wherein ye greatly rejoice, though now for a season, if need be, ye are in heaviness through manifold temptations:

That the trial of your faith, being much more precious than of gold that perisheth, though it be tried with fire, might be found unto praise and honour and glory at the appearing of Jesus Christ.

Whom having not seen, ye love; in whom, though now ye see him not, yet believing, ye rejoice with joy unspeakable and full of glory:

Receiving the end of your faith, even the salvation of your souls.

Of which salvation the prophets have enquired and searched diligently, who prophesied of the grace that should come unto you:

Searching what, or what manner of time the Spirit of Christ which was in them did signify, when it testified beforehand the sufferings of Christ, and the glory that should follow.   I Peter 1:5-11

Please note again that the promise of not falling from grace, and thereby securing an entrance into the everlasting kingdom, is based on continuance in growth.

But if we walk in the light, as he is in the light, we have fellowship one with another, and the blood of Jesus Christ his Son cleanseth us from all sin.   I John 1:7

To walk in the light means to obey revealed truth. If we do not walk in the light, the fellowship with God stops, and the blood of Jesus Christ His Son ceases to cleanse us from sin.

Always does this condition of following, continuing, or being obedient, enter the picture of the believers security.

Some are abhorred at the very thought of us having anything to do with our security as a believer. Why can we not see such obvious scriptures concerning this truth?

Having therefore these promises, dearly beloved, let us cleanse ourselves from all filthiness of the flesh and spirit, perfecting holiness in the fear of God. II Corinthians 7:1

Examine yourselves, whether ye be in the faith; prove your own selves. Know ye not your own selves, how that Jesus Christ is in you, except ye be reprobates?

II Corinthians 13:5

Wherefore, my beloved, as ye have always obeyed, not as in my presence only, but now much more in my absence, work out your own salvation with fear and trembling.

Philippians 2:12

If ye then be risen with Christ, seek those things which are above, where Christ sitteth on the right hand of God.

Set your affection on things above, not on things on the earth.

Mortify therefore your members which are upon the earth; fornication, uncleanness, inordinate affection, evil concupiscence, and covetousness, which is idolatry:

For which things' sake the wrath of God cometh on the children of disobedience: Colossians 3:1, 2, 5, 6

Take heed, brethren, lest there be in any of you an evil heart of unbelief, in departing from the living God.

Hebrews 3:12

How can anyone depart from the living God if they were not with Him?

Let us holdfast the profession of our faith without wavering; (for he is faithful that promised;)   Hebrews 10:23

But ye, beloved, building up yourselves on your most holy faith, praying in the Holy Ghost,

Keep yourselves *in the love of God, looking for the mercy of our Lord Jesus Christ unto eternal life.* Jude 20, 21

Many are confused about the difference between works and sin. They think that to abstain from sin is trusting in our good works to get us to heaven. This is not so!

For by grace are ye saved through faith; and that not of

yourselves: it is the gift of God:
Not of works, lest any man should boast.

Ephesians 2:8, 9

The fact that we cannot be saved by our own good works is beyond dispute to the true child of God. We can never make ourselves good enough to save ourselves. We must come as a sinner, as one hymn writer put it:

Nothing in my hand I bring, Simply to Thy cross I cling.

It is after we are born again, that works begin.

For we are his workmanship, created in Christ Jesus unto good works, which God hath before ordained that we should walk in them.

Ephesians 2:10

So many have misinterpreted I Corinthians 3:10-15 to mean that if we have sin in our lives, we will still go to heaven, but our rewards will be lost. Paul is not talking about sins, he is talking of working carnal works with a carnal motive.

Sinners do not enter heaven as saints. Sinners cannot inherit eternal life.

*Know ye not that the unrighteous **shall not** inherit the kingdom of God? Be not deceived: neither fornicators, nor idolaters, nor adulterers, nor effeminate, nor abusers of themselves with mankind.*

Not thieves, nor covetous, nor drunkards, nor revilers, nor extortioners, shall inherit the kingdom of God.

I Corinthians 6:9, 10

Oh, what a disastrous mistake to believe we can be saved and continue to practice sin, and then inherit eternal life.

Now the works of the flesh are manifest, which are these; Adultery, fornication, uncleanness, lasciviousness,

Idolatry, witchcraft, hatred, variance, emulations, wrath, strife, seditions, heresies,

*Envyings murders, drunkenness, revellings, and such like: of the which I tell you before, as I have also told you in time past, that they which do such things **shall not** inherit the kingdom of God.*

Galatians 5:19-21

131

Just today, the same day I am writing this chapter, I read in the religious magazine of an internationally known T.V. evangelist the following words, and I quote, "In attempting to define holiness, there is the tendency to look at a person, an individual, and this is error. **There is no such thing as personal holiness.** Any measure of holiness we may have is because God has chosen to give it to us, freely and as a gift. **It is all of God — and none of us.**"

How can this brilliant man miss so many scripture references that prove part of holiness is our doing?

Having therefore these promises, dearly beloved, let us cleanse ourselves from all filthiness of the flesh and spirit, perfecting holiness in the fear of God.

II Corinthians 7:1

Wherefore gird up the loins of your mind, be sober, and hope to the end for the grace that is to be brought unto you at the revelation of Jesus Christ;

As obedient children, not fashioning yourselves according to the former lusts in your ignorance:

But as he which hath called you is holy, so be ye holy in all manner of conversation;

Because it is written, Be ye holy; for I am holy.

I Peter 1:13-16

Why does God **command us to be holy** if it is none of our doing?

Then this world-famous evangelist goes on to say, "Even if our conditional holiness doesn't come up to our positional holiness (provided we do not reprobate ourselves) we will still be saved, but our works will be burned."

Can he not see, this Pentecostal minister, that he is teaching eternal security?

I do not point out the preceding to be harsh or unkind but rather, I see the snare in which he is leading millions.

Many times the example is given of our natural children still being our children no matter how evil or wicked they become. After all, we are still their father and they our children. Let me point out a great truth here.

There was a certain rich man, which was clothed in purple and fine linen, and fared sumptuously every day:

And there was a certain beggar named Lazarus, which was laid at his gate, full of sores,

And desiring to be fed with the crumbs which fell from the rich man's table: moreover the dogs came and licked his sores.

And it came to pass, that the beggar died, and was carried by the angels into Abraham's bosom: the rich man also died, and was buried;

And in hell he lift up his eyes, being in torments, and seeth Abraham afar off, and Lazarus in his bosom.

And he cried and said, Father Abraham, have mercy on me, and send Lazarus, that he may dip the tip of his finger in water, and cool my tongue; for I am tormented in this flame.

*But Abraham said. **Son**, remember that thou in thy lifetime receivedst thy good things, and likewise Lazarus evil things: but now he is comforted, and thou art tormented.*

Luke 16:19-25

Please notice, the rich man in hell called Abraham, "Father Abraham." Father Abraham called the rich man, "Son." But, Abraham was still in paradise, and the rich man was still in hell.

Let's stop using foolish, made-up examples to attempt to prove a false doctrine. Let's believe the truth and use the word of God to destroy false doctrine.

(For the weapons of our warfare are not carnal, but mighty through God to the pulling down of strong holds;)

Casting down imaginations, and every high thing that exalteth itself against the knowledge of God, and bringing into captivity every thought to the obedience of Christ;

II Corinthians 10:4, 5

The following are just a few of many scriptures that plainly warn that a person can lose his eternal salvation.

133

If a man abide not in me, he is cast forth as a branch, and is withered; and men gather them, and cast them into the fire, and they are burned.   John 15:6

Because that, when they knew God, they glorified him not as God, neither were thankful; but became vain in their imaginations, and their foolish heart was darkened.

For this cause God gave them up unto vile affections: for even their women did change the natural use into that which is against nature:

And likewise also the men, leaving the natural use of the woman, burned in their lust one toward another; men with men working that which is unseemly, and receiving in themselves that recompence of their error which was meet.

And even as they did not like to retain God in their knowledge. God gave them over to a reprobate mind, to do those things which are not convenient;

Romans 1:21, 26-28

But I keep under my body, and bring it into subjection: lest that by any means, when I have preached to others, I myself should be a castaway.   I Corinthians 9:27

I will therefore that the younger women marry, bear children, guide the house, give none occasion to the adversary to speak reproachfully.

For some are already turned aside after Satan.

I Timothy 5:14,15

If we suffer, we shall also reign with him: if we deny him, he also will deny us: II Timothy 2:12

Brethren, if any of you do err from the truth, and one convert him;

Let him know, that he which converteth the sinner from the error of his way shall save a soul from death, and shall hide a multitude of sins.   James 5:19, 20

For if God spared not the angels that sinned, but cast them down to hell, and delivered them into chains of darkness, to be reserved unto judgement;   II Peter 2:4

*For if after they have escaped the pollutions of the world through the knowledge of the Lord and Saviour Jesus Christ, they are again entangled therein, and overcome, the **latter end is worse** with them than the beginning.*

II Peter 2:20

But the heavens and the earth, which are now, by the same word are kept in store, reserved unto fire against the day of judgement and perdition of ungoldly men.

II Peter 3:7

Those who teach unconditional eternal security would have us believe those who go back into sin were really never saved. I believe that is true in many cases. Some people do not receive a valid conversion experience. Many make a decision, a start, a good start, but are not really born of the Spirit of God. They put on good works, honestly, sincerely. However, because it is human effort, without being born of the Spirit, it will not stand the test.

The fact of the matter is this: when God saves us, as far as He is concerned, we are saved for all eternity. He never intends for us to backslide. Much of the backsliding, or falling away, is the result of the mentality the Church has received through years of negative teaching and preaching.

By negative, I mean the idea that we all have to sin a little every day; that backsliding, or growing cold spiritually, is a normal and expected phase of the Christian life that we cannot help. This teaching is sheer nonsense and is neither scriptural nor intelligent.

So many Christians are living in an up and down, in and out, half-defeated, half-victorious Christian life because of this preaching they have heard, and the lives they have observed have taught them that this is the normal Christian life.

But to teach that you **cannot** be lost is to ignore volumes of scripture.

*Now the Spirit speaketh expressly, that in the latter times some shall **depart from the faith**, giving heed to seducing*

135

spirits, and doctrines of devils; I Timothy 4:1

A person cannot depart from the faith if he has never been in the faith.

Praise God, we can be saved! We can have security! But that security depends on the relationship we maintain with Christ after we are born into God's family.

But if we walk in the light, as he is in the light, we have fellowship one with another, and the blood of Jesus Christ his Son cleanseth us from all sin. I John 1:7

I promise you, God's grace will keep you if you want to be kept. But you must want to be kept.

THE DECISION IS YOURS.

As we said before, so say I now again, If any man preach any other gospel unto you than that ye have received, let him be accursed. Galatians 1:9

Books by William F. Hill

10 Things I Need from God
And He Gave Some Pastors
Choices
Devil, Don't Mess With Me
Evangelism—The Heartbeat of God
Exceeding Abundantly Above with Seize the Day! A
FAITH That Moves Mountains*
From the Table...To the Horse, To the Throne
Fundamental Facts For Faithful Followers*
IF*
Ziklag*
Make to Yourselves Friends of Money*
Poverty Is No Blessing—7 Steps From Poverty to Prosperity* A
Qualities of a Conqueror A
The Husband As...Prophet, Priest, Protector, Provider* A
Debra R. Stacey, Hill's daughter has written a short message to wives at end of each chapter.
Four in One: Spirit Soul Body/The Truth About the Trinity/
Must Christians Keep the Sabbath?/Whores Idols Makeup Jewelry
Two in One: 10 Commandments For Preachers and Christian Workers/
Watching Waiting Weeping Winning
Two in One: Humility and How I Obtained It/I Was Wounded in the House of My Friends
Two in One: The Most Dangerous Sin in America/The Unpardonable Sin
Two in One: The Man With the Pitcher in His Hand/Partners With God
What Is God's Name?*
What Is Holiness?*

*These books have Bible Study Lessons available.

A=Also available in audio CD's, read by the author.

Books by Debra R. Stacey

From My Heart to Yours—
52 Devotions geared especially to those involved in the music ministry.
Abigail—In Adversity and Adventure
Rebekah—A Biblical Novel
The Call to Worship*
The Wife As...Mother, Manager, Model, Matriarch* A
Woman of God—A Vessel of Honor* A

Holiness Literature International
PO Box 263
Independence, IA 50644 USA
www.calvary-center.com   www.holinessliterature.com

Music CD's

Live...In My Father's House—CEC Choir
The Call to Worship—CEC Choir
Hotline to Heaven—CEC Choir
We're Gonna Have Church Tonight—CEC Choir
Calvary Singers Favorites—Calvary Singers
He Always Answers—Debra R. Stacey
Always and Forever—Debra R. Stacey

Made in the USA
Charleston, SC
18 September 2011